WINNIE-THE-POOH ON MANAGEMENT

"Indisputably and intrinsically this tome is a compendium of Machiavellian callidity."
—Owl

"Tiggers don't like haycorns or honey but they love this book."
—Tigger

"People say, 'It's only Eeyore so it doesn't count.' They'll probably skip over the parts about me. But that's all right. I'm still in it."
—Eeyore

"If enough people read this, I may become a VIP."
—Edward Bear

ROGER E. ALLEN is an associate of Allen Associates, a management consulting firm whose clients have included organizations in the fields of public administration, computers, finance, plastics, textiles, forest products and more. Trained as an industrial and mechanical engineer, he gained line management experience with Procter & Gamble, Root Corporation, Deckers Corporation and other prominent companies. He currently lives in University Place, Washington, where he continues to maintain his lifelong friendship with a certain Very Important Bear and friends.

Winnie-the-Pooh

on Management

In which a
Very Important Bear
and his friends
are introduced to a
Very Important Subject

Roger E. Allen

METHUEN

First published in Great Britain 1995
by Methuen London
an imprint of Reed International Books Ltd
Michelin House, 81 Fulham Road, London SW3 6RB
and Auckland, Melbourne, Singapore and Toronto

Reprinted 1995 (twice), 1996 (six times)

A CIP catalogue record for this title
is available from the British Library
ISBN 0 413 69720 7

Typeset in the United States of America
Printed and bound in Great Britain by
Cox & Wyman Ltd, Reading, Berkshire

This book is dedicated to:

Marilyn: my friend, my wife, my love, my life.

Our three sons and their families:
Mark, his wife, Jody, Matt and Scottie
Stephen, his wife, Stasia, Christopher and Thomas
Jeffrey, his wife, Shirley, and Bryce

ACKNOWLEDGMENTS

A book is a collaborative effort, even if the author's name stands alone on the title page. I want to express my appreciation and thanks to those who helped make this book possible.

Winnie-the-Pooh, a Very Important Bear

Steve Allen

Stasia Allen

Marilyn G. Allen

Mark E. Allen

Jeff Allen

Esther J. Allen: my mother, who told me stories and introduced me to Edward Bear

The staff of Dutton, including:

Rachel Klayman and Matthew Carnicelli, my editors; Julie Park, Joan Powers, Lisa Johnson, and others.

And, of course, A. A. Milne, creator of children's classics.

And all the managers, good and bad, with whom I have worked. I learned from every one of you.

CONTENTS

x *Contents*

INTRODUCTION

> . . . Christopher Robin said:
> "What do you like doing best in the world, Pooh?"
> "Well," said Pooh, "what I like best—" and then he
> had to stop and think. Because although Eating Honey was
> a very good thing to do, there was a moment just before you
> began to eat it which was better than when you were, but he
> didn't know what it was called.

If you were reading a good book, that moment might be called an "Introduction." Ideally, it should raise your anticipation, tell you what the book is about, how it came to be written, and why you should read it.

All about us we can see failures of management: unrepaired potholes, high school graduates who can't read or write, cars that need to be recalled, wasted tax dollars, unsafe streets and neighborhoods. The list is long and increases daily. Why is this?

My management experience in both the private and public sector has convinced me that managers need to spend less time and attention on sophisticated approaches to management and devote more time to improving and practicing the six functions of a manager's job. They need to get back to basics.

That is what this book is about—the six functions that a manager should master, and how every manager can do so.

The book is also about A. A. Milne's world of Winnie-the-Pooh. At first it might seem odd to combine a children's classic with management. The purpose of doing so is to explore the six functions in an unfamiliar context, which will allow us to think about them in a new way and make the basics of a manager's job clear and understandable.

If this is to be done, one or more visits to that world would be "REQIRD" (as Owl's door knocker's notice read) to refresh memories of Pooh's adventures and to see what we can learn from them.

It has been a long time since I visited the Forest where Pooh and his friends live. I would be a stranger there to be sure, but I am certain that Pooh will help, being That Kind of Bear.

If you are a manager, there may be some reminders in this book about things you know but haven't thought about recently and some skills that could stand a little honing and polishing.

If you'd like to be a manager but aren't, this is a good place to start.

If you aren't a manager, the skills of a manager can help you manage your own day-to-day activities better.

If you're a significant other, child, spouse, or friend

of a manager, this book can help you to understand the Very Important Job a manager does.

So, follow along on tiptoe to the Forest and see what adventures await. Don't worry about finding it. After all, A. A. Milne said in his introduction to *The House At Pooh Corner* ". . . the Forest will always be there . . . and anybody who is Friendly with Bears can find it."

Come. . . .

I

IN WHICH Winnie-the-Pooh Learns About Management and What Makes Someone a Manager

That morning Pooh had been looking in the Forest for a bee-tree that might possibly contain honey, when he came up behind a stranger standing still and looking as if he might be lost.

Pooh had had some experience in being lost the time they had tried to unBounce Tigger. He knew how offputting it could be when you've missed your way somehow, so he spoke up nicely.

"Hallo," he said in his best I-know-where-I-am voice, just to be reassuring. "I'm Edward Bear. Can I help you?"

The Stranger turned around, stopped looking lost, and looked pleased. "Good morning, Pooh. I was hoping to find you so that you could. Help me, that is."

"How could I help you?" asked Pooh.

"Well." The Stranger put down the picnic basket he

had been holding. "I'm writing a book, and it seemed to me that if you let me write about some of the adventures you and your friends have had, it would be a better book. It's a book about management."

"Man-age-ment," said Edward Bear in the somewhat puzzled tone he used when he was thinking, or, as Eeyore might say, "Trying to think."

"Yes. Management."

"That is a very long word." Pooh reflected. "It is the kind of long word that Owl uses. Does it stand for something good, like ah ummm honey?"

"Well, not exactly. It stands for something that some people called managers do. Management is neither good nor bad. It just is. You can have either good or bad management, depending on how managers do their job."

"That seems very confusing. Almost everyone I know thinks that honey is good always."

"Yes. Well, we are not talking about honey."

"I am." Pooh rubbed his tummy. "In fact, I was looking for some but I found you instead."

"We are talking about management."

"I'd rather talk about honey. Before you came along, I thought I heard a buzzing-noise. Why don't we walk down to the old hollow tree and see if the buzzing-noise came from some bees that just might be making honey?"

"We can go down there later, but first I want to talk

about management because it's a Very Important Subject and I think you can help me, if you will."

Pooh cast a lingering look in the direction of the bees that were making the buzzing-noise and then brightened. "If it's a Very Important Subject, and I help you with it, then I might have a chance to become a Very Important Bear."

"That's quite possible. Shall we sit down and talk about it?"

"Bother! I'd really like some honey, but I suppose, that if I want to become a V.I.B., I shall have to." Pooh carefully selected a comfortable-looking stone that had an unobstructed view of the old hollow bee-tree and sat down. "We can talk and at the same time keep an eye on the tree just in case anyone else heard a buzzing-noise and decided to come to see if it came from some bees that might be making honey."

"All right. Now, the reason that management is a Very Important Subject is that if we didn't have management, most important things wouldn't get done, or if they did, they wouldn't get done very well."

"Like going to visit Rabbit and his not having remembered to stock his larder with a pot of honey to put on the bread that he should serve to guests who just happen to drop by and might like to have a mouthful of something?"

"Exactly. That and many other important things."

Pooh sat up straight, taking more of an interest in

the subject of management. "So why don't people who management—"

"—people who manage—"

"—manage learn how to do it properly?"

"That's the problem. Just about everybody agrees on what management is. 'The art and science of directing effort and resources so that the established objectives of an enterprise may be attained in accordance with accepted policies' is one definition. It is the 'How' that nobody is quite sure about."

Pooh nodded, assuming his wise-bear look. "*How* is difficult," he said. "If you ask Eeyore how he is, he almost always says, 'Not very how.' Everyone has trouble with 'How.' I remember once when I heard a buzzing-noise from the top of a tree and decided that there might be honey there. I also decided that I would like to eat a little honey. It was the 'How' to get the honey that was troublesome."

"Well, it is the same thing with management. It seems that almost everyone has a theory about good management and how it can be achieved. There are stacks and stacks of books on the subject. There are books on Theory X and Theory Y and I think even on Theory Z. There are books called *Eupsychian Management* by Abraham Maslow; *The Practice of Management* by Peter Drucker; *Creative Management* by Shigeru Kobayashi; *In Search of Excellence* by Thomas J. Peters and Robert H. Waterman Jr.; *The One-Minute Manager* by Kenneth Blanchard and Spencer Johnson; and on and on and on. They are good books, but—"

"—but they sound very complicated," said Pooh.

"That is why I came to you. Over the past twenty years or so, I think that many managers have been distracted by the theories in these books and by management fads. They have paid too much attention to trying the latest management theory and not enough attention to the real basics of managing. I think that most would improve their performance tremendously by concentrating on these basics of a manager's job.

"I think that many of your adventures illustrate those basic functions of a manager that, if practiced consistently and properly, would help any manager do a really excellent job."

"They would?" Pooh sounded surprised. "Oh, yes. They would," he said in a barely certain kind of voice.

"For instance, the adventure you mentioned—when you tried to get honey—could be used as a good example of the six basic functions in the work of a manager. Those are the things that are common to all managers and what makes them managers rather than something else."

"You mean a manager instead of—say—a bee?" Pooh stared off in the direction of a tree. "I thought I heard a buzzing-sound just then."

The Stranger listened carefully. "I think someone in the village on the far side of the Forest is running a stick along a picket fence."

"Oh. I thought it might have been a bee."

"No. I think it just sounded like a bee."

"I see." Then to show that he had been paying attention, Pooh asked, "What are the six functions of a manager's job?"

"Let's use your adventure of getting the honey to identify them," suggested The Stranger. He opened the picnic basket, took out a little morning snack of something that he kindly gave to Pooh, and then took out a book, which he leafed through until he found the place he wanted. "I believe it went like this." The Stranger began to read.

> One day when he was out walking, he came to an open place in the middle of the forest, and in the middle of this place was a large oak-tree, and, from the top of the tree, there came a loud buzzing-noise.
>
> Winnie-the-Pooh sat down at the foot of the tree, put his head between his paws and began to think.
>
> First of all he said to himself: "That buzzing-noise

means something. You don't get a buzzing-noise like that, just buzzing and buzzing, without its meaning something. If there's a buzzing-noise, somebody's making a buzzing-noise, and the only reason for making a buzzing-noise that *I* know of is because you're a bee."

Then he thought another long time, and said:

"And the only reason for being a bee that I know of is making honey."

And then he got up, and said: "And the only reason for making honey is so as *I* can eat it." So he began to climb the tree. . . .

Then as he climbed a little further . . . and a little further . . . and then just a little further. . . .

He was getting rather tired by this time, so that is why he sang a Complaining Song. He was nearly there now, and if he just stood on that branch . . .

Crack! . . .

"It all comes, I suppose," he decided, as he said good-bye to the last branch, spun round three times, and flew gracefully into a gorse-bush, "it all comes of *liking* honey so much. Oh, help!"

He crawled out of the gorse-bush, brushed the prickles from his nose, and began to think again. And the first person he thought of was Christopher Robin. . . .

So Winnie-the-Pooh went round to his friend Christopher Robin, who lived behind a green door in another part of the forest.

"Good morning, Christopher Robin," he said.

"Now, that illustrates the first function a manager should perform, which is Establishing Objectives," said

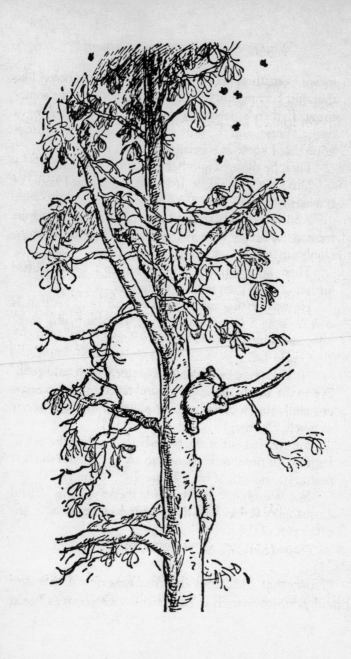

The Stranger. "It is also the first thing she should do for the operation she is managing."

Pooh looked puzzled. "Are managers always 'shes'?" he asked.

"No," The Stranger answered. "Many are hes. You see, pronouns are difficult. The convention of using the male pronoun when referring to a situation that could involve either is confusing and annoys some people. Therefore, when I'm writing or talking, I sometimes use the male pronoun and sometimes the female pronoun, which is what I did here."

Pooh nodded, to show he understood, but he really didn't. "If Christopher Robin were here, he would write the first function with a stick here in this patch of earth, because it sounds like something to be remembered. I'd do it, but he is the only one in the Forest who can spell."

"A good idea. I'll do it as we talk." The Stranger picked up a stick and wrote in the dirt in big letters.

THE SIX FUNCTIONS IN THE WORK OF A MANAGER

1. ESTABLISHING OBJECTIVES

"This was the first thing you did when you noticed the bee-tree. You decided that you wanted to get the honey, and how much of it you wanted."

"All of it," said Pooh wistfully.

"You then went to Christopher Robin whose help was needed to attain the goal and meet the objective." The Stranger continued to read:

"I wonder if you've got such a thing as a balloon about you?"

"A balloon?"

"Yes, I just said to myself coming along: 'I wonder if Christopher Robin has such a thing as a balloon about him?' I just said it to myself, thinking of balloons, and wondering."

"What do you want a balloon for?" you said.

Winnie-the-Pooh looked round to see that nobody was listening, put his paw to his mouth, and said in a deep whisper: *"Honey!"*

"But you don't get honey with balloons!"

"I do," said Pooh. . . .

Well, you both went out with the blue balloon, and you took your gun with you, just in case, as you always did, and Winnie-the-Pooh went to a very muddy place that he knew of, and rolled and rolled until he was black all over; and then, when the balloon was blown up as big as big, and you and Pooh were both holding on to the string, you let go suddenly, and Pooh Bear floated gracefully up into the sky, and stayed there—level with the top of the tree and about twenty feet away from it.

"That was very good, Pooh," said The Stranger. "You effectively carried out the second function that a good manager performs." Under the first function The Stranger wrote:

2. ORGANIZING

"You analyzed what had to be done in order to reach the objectives. You determined what resources you would need, what jobs needed to be performed, and who would be best suited to do the required work. You made that assignment based on your evaluation of their talents and abilities."

"Christopher Robin had a balloon and a gun just in case something should go wrong and they were needed."

"Exactly. He was best because Rabbit, or Piglet, or Eeyore didn't have those things. Once you had picked Christopher Robin, you went on to the third function, which is Motivating." The Stranger wrote that down as number three.

3. MOTIVATING

"What's moti—motiva—whatever?" asked Pooh.

"Motivating. It means the reason why someone would want to do something. If you, as a manager, want someone to do a job or to help you accomplish an objective, you must find a reason why he or she should help and tell him or her what it is."

"I told Christopher Robin about the honey."

"Since you knew he liked honey, that gave him a reason or a motive to help you get it. He knew that if he helped, he would share it when you achieved your objective. You were motivating him to help you."

"Almost everybody likes Honey," said Pooh. "But it seems to me that there might be another reason. Christopher Robin is always willing to do something to help me, even if there is no honey. I think it's because I'm his favorite bear."

"Excellent," The Stranger complimented him. "Liking someone else can be the strongest motivator of all. That was very astute of you."

"That Kind of Bear!" thought Pooh, although he didn't say it out loud. "What is the fourth function?" he asked instead.

"Developing people. A good manager must make certain to do this, although it is easy to neglect." The Stranger wrote it down.

4. DEVELOPING PEOPLE

"That was what you were doing when you were being a cloud and you were coaching Christopher Robin in how he should act to make the bees think that you were a cloud and not a bear hanging from a balloon. You remember, it went like this."

"Christopher Robin!"

"Yes?"

"Have you an umbrella in your house?"

"I think so."

"I wish you would bring it out here, and walk up and down with it, and look up at me every now and then, and say 'Tut-tut, it looks like rain.' I think, if you did that, it would help the deception which we are practising on these bees."

Well, you laughed to yourself, "Silly old Bear!" but you didn't say it aloud because you were so fond of him, and you went home for your umbrella.

"Oh, there you are!" called down Winnie-the-Pooh, as soon as you got back to the tree. "I was beginning to get anxious. I have discovered that the bees are now definitely Suspicious."

"Shall I put my umbrella up?" you said.

"Yes, but wait a moment. We must be practical. The important bee to deceive is the Queen Bee. Can you see which is the Queen Bee from down there?"

"No."

"A pity. Well, now, if you walk up and down with your umbrella, saying, 'Tut-tut, it looks like rain,' I shall do what I can by singing a little Cloud Song, such as a cloud might sing. . . . Go!"

So, while you walked up and down and wondered if it would rain, Winnie-the-Pooh sang this song:

> *How sweet to be a Cloud*
> > *Floating in the Blue!*
> *Every little cloud*
> *Always sings aloud.*

> *"How sweet to be a Cloud*
> > *Floating in the Blue!"*
> *It makes him very proud*
> *To be a little cloud.*

"You mean when he had put his umbrella up and was walking up and down, and I told him he should say 'Tut, tut, tut, it looks like rain'?"

"Exactly. You were developing his acting ability. What is more, you developed your own 'cloudness' by singing a little Cloud Song."

"Yes." Pooh nodded. "I thought it was one of my better Cloud Songs, but I'm not sure that the bees thought so."

"Well, improvement in performance usually comes in stages. Perhaps next time they will think so. Now here is a great example of the fifth function." The Stranger read from the book.

"Christopher Robin!" he said in a loud whisper.

"Hallo!"

"I think the bees *suspect* something!"

"What sort of thing?"

"I don't know. But something tells me that they're *suspicious*!"

"Perhaps they think that you're after their honey."

"It may be that. You never can tell with bees." . . .

The bees were still buzzing as suspiciously as ever. Some of them, indeed, left their nest and flew all round the cloud as it began the second verse of this song, and one bee sat down on the nose of the cloud for a moment, and then got up again.

"Christopher—*ow!*—Robin," called out the cloud.

"Yes?"

"I have just been thinking, and I have come to a very important decision. *These are the wrong sort of bees.*"

The Stranger wrote down COMMUNICATING as number five.

5. COMMUNICATING

"Communicating is just telling everyone who has something to do with your project what is going on," said The Stranger. "It's something that happens when you tell them things, and also it has to do with the way you act and work with them."

"Like telling Christopher Robin that the bees were definitely suspicious."

"Yes, and you were also communicating when you said '*ow!*' when the bee stung the nose of the cloud."

"That wasn't meant to be communication," said Pooh, remembering and rubbing the nose of the cloud.

"Nevertheless, it was effective and gave a member of your team information about the true state of the situation, which is what communication is supposed to do."

"That's nice to know. At the time it wasn't so nice."

"I can imagine. Now, the sixth thing that a manager must do is to establish measures of how things are, both in terms of progress toward the objective and in how each individual is doing—her performance, in other words.

"That is called Measurement and Analysis. Remember, you did it this way":

> "Christopher Robin, you must shoot the balloon with your gun. Have you got your gun?"
>
> "Of course I have," you said. "But if I do that, it will spoil the balloon," you said.
>
> "But if you *don't*," said Pooh, "I shall have to let go, and that would spoil *me*."
>
> When you put it like this, you saw how it was, and you aimed very carefully at the balloon, and fired.
>
> "*Ow!*" said Pooh.
>
> "Did I miss?" you asked.
>
> "You didn't exactly *miss*," said Pooh, "but you missed the *balloon*."
>
> "I'm so sorry," you said, and you fired again, and this time you hit the balloon, and the air came slowly out, and Winnie-the-Pooh floated down to the ground.

The Stranger wrote:

6. MEASUREMENT AND ANALYSIS

"This is possibly one of the most important factors, because unless individuals know how they are doing and what they are doing correctly, they can't improve their performance. Of course, the results of your measurement must be communicated to everyone on the team.

"You were doing exactly this, Pooh, when you told Christopher Robin that his first shot had missed the balloon. And by telling him what his first shot hit, you enabled him to correct his aim and improve his performance with his second shot."

"I'm glad I did that," said Pooh. "I think."

"Managers are always glad when someone on their team improves their performance."

Pooh was not so certain that he would improve his performance the next time he tried to get honey from the bee-tree unless he did something very different. He climbed down from his rock, walked over, and stood looking at the list of the six functions in the work of a manager to see if they gave him any ideas on how to get the honey that he was almost certain was in the tree where he could hear the buzzing-noise.

THE SIX FUNCTIONS IN THE WORK OF A MANAGER

1. **ESTABLISHING OBJECTIVES**
2. **ORGANIZING**
3. **MOTIVATING**
4. **DEVELOPING PEOPLE**
5. **COMMUNICATING**
6. **MEASUREMENT AND ANALYSIS**

Except they didn't quite look like that because in getting to where he could see them, he had walked across them, so they looked more like this:

1.   ABLISH   OBJECTIVES
2. ORG   ZING
3. MOTI   ING
4. DEVELOP   OPLE
5. COMMUNI   ING
6. MEASUR   ENT AND ANALYSIS

Pooh stood looking down for a while. Finally he said, "What's an 'ENT' that a manager's supposed to measure?"

"It's supposed to be 'MEASUREMENT.' You walked across the list and scuffed out some of the letters."

"Oh. I didn't think we had talked about anything like an 'ENT.' To tell the truth, I was also wondering a little about 'OPLE.' Now I see. But there is one other thing that I don't understand."

"What's that?"

Pooh pointed at the list. "These all look like 'Whats.' It's the 'Hows' that I have trouble with."

"That's very true. However, before we could work on the 'Hows,' we first had to know what the 'Whats' were that the 'Hows' would apply to."

"I see," said Pooh in a puzzled tone of voice that sounded as if he really weren't sure. "Shall we start on the 'Hows'?"

The Stranger looked up at the sun. "It seems to me that it's well past lunchtime. I think we've talked enough for one day. Shall we go down and see if that really was a buzzing-noise made by bees making honey, or would you rather go back to where I left a picnic basket, which I happen to know has a large pot of honey inside it?"

II

IN WHICH Pooh Visits Owl in the
Hundred Acre Wood, Has Management
Theories Explained, and Fears He Is
a Bear of No Brain at All

Pooh was puzzled. Actually, he wasn't so much puzzled as he was confuzzled. Confuzzled was almost the longest word that Pooh knew, and he hadn't known that until Christopher Robin had explained that it meant sort of mixed up and baffled.

Pooh had been feeling confuzzled ever since he had talked to The Stranger about management. It had been a Very Nice Conversation and Pooh had particularly liked the way it ended with the very large pot of honey that The Stranger had thoughtfully brought along in the picnic basket.

Pooh had understood very well about what management was and about the six basic functions in the work of a manager, particularly after The Stranger had mentioned that Pooh had scuffed out some of the letters when he had walked around to look at the list The

Stranger had written in the dirt. That part seemed very simple and easy to understand, even for a Bear of Very Little Brain.

Which was what was confuzzling. It all seemed very simple, except the "How" perhaps, but The Stranger had said that stacks and stacks of books had been written about the theories of management and had named some of them. If it seemed simple, why had so many books been written? Perhaps he, Pooh, didn't really understand, after all.

It was a fine spring morning in the forest as he started out. Little soft clouds played happily in a blue sky, skipping from time to time in front of the sun as if they had come to put it out, and then sliding away suddenly so that the next might have his turn. Through them and between them the sun shone bravely; and a copse which had worn its firs all the year round seemed old and dowdy now beside the new green lace which the beeches had put on so prettily. Through copse and spinney marched Bear; down open slopes of gorse and heather, over rocky beds of streams, up steep banks of sandstone into the heather again; and so at last, tired and hungry, to the Hundred Acre Wood. For it was in the Hundred Acre Wood that Owl lived.

"And if anyone knows anything about anything," said Bear to himself, "it's Owl who knows something about something," he said, "or my name's not Winnie-the-Pooh," he said. "Which it is," he added. "So there you are."

Owl lived at The Chestnuts, an old-world residence of great charm, which was grander than anybody else's, or seemed so to Bear, because it had both a knocker *and* a bell-pull. Underneath the knocker there was a notice which said:

PLES RING IF AN RNSER IS REQIRD.

Underneath the bell-pull there was a notice which said:

PLEZ CNOKE IF AN RNSR IS NOT REQID.

These notices had been written by Christopher Robin, who was the only one in the forest who could spell; for Owl, wise though he was in many ways, able to read and write and spell his own name WOL, yet somehow went all to pieces over delicate words like MEASLES and BUTTERED TOAST.

Winnie-the-Pooh read the two notices very carefully, first from left to right, and afterwards, in case he had missed some of it, from right to left. Then, to make quite sure, he knocked and pulled the knocker, and he pulled and knocked the bell-rope, and he called out in a very loud voice, "Owl! I require an answer! It's Bear speaking." And the door opened, and Owl looked out.

"Hallo, Pooh," he said. "How's things?"

"Confuzzled," said Pooh. "And I thought you could help me. About management, that is."

"Well," said Owl. "That's a Very Serious Subject and might take awhile. Could you stay for lunch?"

"I think I could stay that long," said Pooh, trying to see over Owl's shoulder if his larder was as well stocked as usual. "Nothing elaborate though. Just a mouthful of condensed milk or whatnot, with perhaps a lick of honey—unless, of course, you have a pot of honey that is old and just might spoil soon unless somebody who wanted to do a favor finished it off. In which case, I would help—finish it off, that is."

Owl moved out of the door. "Come in then. Just let me put *The Wall Street Journal* I was reading to one side and we can begin."

"With lunch, I hope," said Pooh. "By the way, I see that my friend Eeyore has lost his tail again."

"Eh?" Owl looked out the door. "I don't see Eeyore out there."

"I meant the bell-rope. The last time I saw it Eeyore was attached to it."

Owl peered at the bell-rope. "Oh, yes. Well, I can see why he would be. I'm rather fond of it myself. It lends a certain air of distinction to my entrance. Actually, it looks remarkably like the one I had previously. Someone unhooked it and took it away just after you visited here that time you were looking for Eeyore's tail. I found this one in the Forest on a bush, just like the last one. It must be that someone is manufacturing them and then being careless when they go through the Forest to market."

"Oh," said Pooh. "I hadn't thought of that."

"Yes. Well, let's sit down and get started."

"With lunch," said Pooh quickly. "Or perhaps we could start with elevenses," he said, glancing at the clock ticking away on Owl's mantelpiece. "I generally have a little something at eleven o'clock in the morning, and it's almost that now."

"Why, so it is," said Owl. "I generally have something myself."

"And then we could have lunch later."

After they had both had a little something, and then had lunch, Owl and Pooh settled down on either side of the fireplace. It was getting blusterous outside, but Owl's house was well constructed, and the fire danced and crackled and threw off a nice warm glow.

Pooh felt that this was a very good place to learn about management theory.

"Well, Pooh," said Owl. "Where shall we start?"

"I don't know," said Pooh. "Since I don't know anything about management theory—except," he said hastily, lest Owl think he was a Bear of Very Little Brain, "what somebody does that makes him a manager instead of, say, a bee—or something else."

"I wasn't asking you the question," said Owl. "I was asking myself."

"I thought you were asking me. I distinctly heard you say, 'Well, Pooh, where shall we start?'"

"That was just a manner of speaking, like when you say to Piglet, 'Isn't it a beautiful day?' You don't really expect an answer because he can see it is a beautiful day."

"Oh," said Pooh. "I see."

"Good," said Owl, relieved that that had been cleared up. "Now, where shall we begin?"

Forgetting that Owl was probably asking himself the question, Pooh said, "I've always found that a good place to begin is at the beginning, because otherwise things can get very confuzzled. If you begin at the end, it's not very interesting, because you already know how things ended before you begin, and if you begin at the middle, you can't go both ways at the same time, and—"

"We will," pronounced Owl firmly, "begin at the beginning."

"Good," said Pooh, and scrunched back in his chair to be in the proper listening position and to get more comfortable.

"One of the earliest records we have about management theory," continued Owl, "is in the eighteenth chapter of Exodus in the Bible. Moses was the leader of a tribe of people called the Israelites."

Owl paused and peered at Pooh. "As you know, it is desirable that a manager be a leader." Pooh nodded to show that he knew that, although he hadn't, really. Not until Owl said it.

"Anyway, Moses was having trouble doing a good job because he was trying to do everything. His father-in-law, Jethro, seeing what was happening, told Moses to pick out some good people and let them handle some of the less important work. This would give Moses more time to do the really important parts of his job. Doing that is called 'Delegation,' and it is a very Important and Necessary thing for a manager to do, even today."

Pooh said "Del-e-ga-tion" to himself several times so that he would remember to ask The Stranger about where it fit into the six functions of a manager's job. It sounded as if it just might be a "How."

He also made up a little Manager Song so he would remember to ask The Stranger about a leader.

The manager, manager,
A leader should be.
That's Most Important,
As we all can see.

He hummed it under his breath until Owl looked at him and asked him if the lunch had not agreed with him because he was making a strange sound.

Pooh said that he was fine and it was a very good lunch, indeed. The sound was just a sound he made when he was trying to remember something.

"Good," said Owl. "Now, the Exodus happened a long time ago, but, ever since then, people have thought about management and have been writing about it."

"That's what The Stranger said. He said there were books about Theory X and Theory Y and Theory Z and lots of others that I forget right now."

And then Pooh had to stop and tell Owl about The Stranger and what he had said. After he had finished, Owl nodded wisely.

"I think we can skip over a lot of the in-between things about management and talk about the more recent theories, like X and Y."

"Good," said Pooh. He rather liked the idea of Theory X because "X" was one of the letters that he knew he could make. You just took two sticks that were the same size and put one on top of the other so that their middles touched.

You had to be careful how you did it, because you might get something that Christopher Robin said was a PLUS sign, which meant something completely different from "X."

Pooh also liked "X" because it was the first letter of a lot of words that meant good things, like Xcellent, Xciting, Xceptional (the kind of Bear Christopher Robin said that he was), and Xtremely delicious, like honey.

Sometimes, when nobody was around, Pooh would make an "X" when he found two of the right-size sticks in the Forest, just to remind himself about "X."

"X and Y," Owl went on, "were what Douglas McGregor, in his book, *The Human Side of Enterprise*, called the two basic choices for managing the worker and working.

"Theory X was the traditional approach, and it assumes that people are lazy and shiftless, work only because they have no choice, dislike working, and have to be driven. It also assumes that people can't take responsibility for themselves and their actions and have to be looked after.

"Theory Y, on the other hand—"

"Why is it on the other hand?" interrupted Pooh.

"What! What?" asked Owl.

"Why is Theory Y on the other hand? I didn't know that Theory X was on the first hand."

"Oh, I see," said Owl. "That is just a way of saying

'as distinguished from' the first thing we were talking about."

"I see," said Pooh, although he didn't. This management theory was difficult to understand sometimes.

"As I was saying, before I was interrupted"—Owl peered sternly at Pooh—"Theory Y assumes that people have a need to work and that they want to do things and take responsibility. They don't want somebody to take care of them. They want to do it themselves.

"As you can see, Pooh, the two theories are exactly opposite. The question is, which one is right? McGregor, who wrote the book, pretended to be impartial, but there was little question that he felt that Theory Y was the way to manage work and workers."

Owl peered at Pooh. "Which one do you think is right?" he asked.

Pooh thought about the two theories until he was sure he had them straight in his mind. Then he thought about all the things he and his friends had done that needed managing. Then he thought about all his friends and everyone he knew. Then he thought about himself.

He thought so long and so hard that he finally thought that he probably needed Strengthening, which he just happened to mention to Owl.

Owl said it was almost teatime anyway, and although he didn't have any of Roo's Strengthening Medicine, perhaps a little more condensed milk and honey on bread might serve the purpose.

"That is possible," said Pooh. "Anyway, it is worth trying."

So they each had a little something, although Pooh's little something was a little more than Owl's little something. Still, when he had licked off the last little bit of honey from the plate, Pooh did feel considerably strengthened.

While Owl cleaned up the dishes and poked up the fire, because it was getting chilly and late in the day, Pooh thought some more.

Finally he shook his head. "I fear I am a Bear of No Brain at All! I can't decide which one is right and which one is wrong. The theories are exactly the opposite; if one is right, then the other must be wrong. It seems to me that some, like Eeyore, would be happier with Theory X and others, like Rabbit, would like Theory Y better. As for myself, sometimes I need taking care of and sometimes I don't. If someone needed taking care of, then Theory Y would not be at all Nice for them."

"Congratulations, Pooh," said Owl. "That is exactly the conclusion that Abraham H. Maslow came to in his book, *Eupsychian Management*. Peter Drucker, who is recognized as an expert in management, concluded that the question is not which theory is right, but that each manager must decide what is right for her own situation. He also said that a new theory is needed because neither Theory X nor Theory Y seem to work very well in all organizations.

"So you see, Pooh, you are not a Bear of No Brain at All. You came to the same conclusion as did some very smart people who are experts in management."

THAT sort of Bear! thought Pooh, feeling much better although still a little confuzzled. He stood up. "Thank you, Owl, for explaining things to me. I had better be leaving now because it is getting late, and it seems to be more blusterous outside than it was."

"Any time at all, Pooh," said Owl as he opened the door. "It is always a pleasure to discuss Very Serious Subjects."

It was very blusterous indeed, and besides he had a feeling that it must be getting close to supper time, so Pooh hurried toward home, jumping down the banks of creeks and bending over to miss low-hanging branches instead of going around.

Still, when he saw the Old Grey Donkey, Eeyore, standing in a thistly corner of the Forest, he thought about the bell-pull at Owl's, slowed down, and went over to him.

"And how are you?" said Winnie-the-Pooh.
Eeyore shook his head from side to side.

"Not very how," he said. "I don't seem to have felt at all how for a long time."

"Dear, dear," said Pooh, "I'm sorry about that. Let's have a look at you."

So Eeyore stood there, gazing sadly at the ground, and Winnie-the-Pooh walked all round him once.

"Why, what's happened to your tail?" he said in surprise.

"What *has* happened to it?" said Eeyore.

"It isn't there!"

"Are you sure?"

"Well, either a tail *is* there or it isn't there. You can't make a mistake about it. And yours *isn't* there!"

"Then what is?"

"Nothing."

"Let's have a look," said Eeyore, and he turned slowly round to the place where his tail had been a little while ago, and then, finding that he couldn't catch it up, he turned round the other way, until he came back to where he was at first, and then he put his head down and looked between his front legs, and at last he said, with a long, sad sigh, "I believe you're right."

"Of course I'm right," said Pooh.

"How like it not to be there," said Eeyore gloomily. "It wasn't there once before, you know."

"Yes, but I think I know where it is, this time. It's at Owl's pretending to be a bell-rope."

"How Strange," said Eeyore. "Some are never satisfied to be What They Are but always want to be Something Else."

"If you go to Owl and ask him, he probably would give it back to you since he has a knocker already. But be sure to ask him nicely, because he said he was fond of it."

"I could tell him that I was attached to it," said Eeyore. "That might convince him, but I doubt it. Oh, well, I might as well try. Thank you, Pooh."

And Eeyore set off in the direction of Owl's house.

"Well," said Pooh to himself, since Eeyore had already left, "at least I think I was right that there are some people who need to be taken care of, sometimes."

III

IN WHICH The Stranger, Pooh, and
Rabbit Talk About the "Hows" of Setting
Objectives and Organizing and Pooh
Forgets to Sing His Manager Song

Sometimes Pooh thought that Rabbit was almost as
Bouncy as Tigger. At other times, he thought that
in Bounciness, nobody could quite come up to Tigger.
Not Rabbit. Not even Kanga. The thing was, Kanga's and Rabbit's Bounciness was a controlled sort of
Bounce, whereas there was no telling just where Tigger's Bounce would land him.

So Pooh was glad it was Rabbit and not Tigger who
came Bouncing along while he was waiting for The
Stranger.

Sometimes Tigger forgot that he had been un-
Bounced, and that might put The Stranger off if he
wasn't expecting to be Bounced on.

"Hallo, Rabbit," said Pooh.

"Good morning, Pooh," said Rabbit. "What are you
doing?"

"Thinking about being a V.I.B. and waiting for The Stranger." And then Pooh had to explain about The Stranger and management and the chance to become a Very Important Bear and everything.

"I see," said Rabbit, when Pooh had finished. "That sounds very interesting."

"Why don't you stay?" asked Pooh. He remembered that Rabbit was one of the smarter and more educated ones in the Forest, and it might be nice for The Stranger to have him there. He also remembered about Motivation and quickly mentioned that The Stranger had had some Very Fine Looking snacks in his picnic basket last time.

"That's not to say that it is certain that he will bring along another picnic basket today, but since he did before, he just might again and very kindly offer to share."

Rabbit didn't have to answer the question, because

just then The Stranger came along through the Forest carrying a picnic basket. Pooh made the introductions and The Stranger and Rabbit said the kind of things that everyone says when they are being introduced. When it was all done, it seemed to be taken for granted that Rabbit would stay.

Then, of course, Pooh had to tell The Stranger about his conversation with Owl about management theory.

"It sounds to me as if Owl did a very good job telling you about those management theories," The Stranger said when Pooh had finished. "I also think that your comments were addressing the really important issue, that of differences. You are very insightful, Pooh."

At that, Pooh felt very good, and he even stopped wondering if there was another pot of honey in the picnic basket that The Stranger had brought.

"You see, if we stop to think about it, we all know that the same individual will react differently under different circumstances and conditions. We also know that each of us is different in our nature, in what we like and don't like, and in our outlook on life and what we want to get from it."

"Rabbit likes to have bread and condensed milk with his honey, but I don't mind just honey," said Pooh, looking at the picnic basket. "I just thought I'd mention that as an example."

"That's a good example. If I had a job that needed

doing and I needed the help of you both, if I offered only fish and chips as a reason for helping, then neither of you might be very interested. Which reminds me, I just happen to have some bread and condensed milk and a pot of honey in my picnic basket, which are more than I can eat. I would really appreciate it if you could both help me when it is time for lunch so that it doesn't spoil."

Pooh and Rabbit both agreed that they would be willing to do that, just so it wouldn't go to waste.

"So," The Stranger continued, "it is difficult to set up one kind of management organization that will work perfectly for everyone. As Peter Drucker says in his book, *Management: Tasks, Responsibilities, Practices,* 'We do not yet have a genuine theory of business and no integrated discipline of business management.' "

"It seems to me then," said Rabbit, who had been listening very carefully, "if that is the case, it makes the manager's job a difficult one."

"It does. But still, it is the manager's responsibility to meet her objectives, so she has to do the best with what she has. She must decide what the reality of her situation is and work with that."

"If Eeyore was here," said Pooh, "he would say that is Discouraging and Sad."

"Not totally. We can look at companies and organizations like Procter & Gamble, 3M, Microsoft, and others that have done a very good job over the years by looking clearly at reality and structuring the way they operate so that they and most of their people perform very well, in spite of there not being an adequate management theory available to them."

"But what about the manager who doesn't work for one of those organizations?" asked Rabbit. "What is he to do?"

"I think the most important thing he can do is to pay regular and careful attention to doing the very best job he possibly can on carrying out the six basic functions of a manager," said The Stranger.

"You see, in this area, the manager has almost complete control of how and what he does. He might not be able, for instance, to have his company change over to a system like 3M's, and indeed it might not be practical or even possible, but he can improve his own performance as a manager.

"In addition, although our knowledge about human nature and management theory is inadequate, we do know quite a bit about the six functions of a manager's job."

"It's the 'Hows' that are difficult," said Pooh.

"Well," said The Stranger, "why don't we take one of your adventures and look at it and see what sort of 'Hows' we can find about the first two basic functions: Establishing Objectives and Organizing."

"Good," said Pooh. "I always like to start at the beginning."

"Since Rabbit is here, what about using an adventure that the two of you shared? Can you think of one that had establishing objectives and organizing as part of it?"

"What about the time Kanga and Baby Roo came to the Forest?" asked Rabbit.

"That might be a very good choice," said The Stranger thoughtfully. "Now, let me see, how did that start?"

Nobody seemed to know where they came from, but there they were in the Forest: Kanga and Baby Roo. When Pooh asked Christopher Robin, "How did they come here?" Christopher Robin said, "In the Usual Way, if you know what I mean, Pooh," and Pooh, who didn't, said "Oh!" Then he nodded his head twice and said, "In the Usual Way. Ah!" Then he went to call upon his friend Piglet to see what *he* thought about it. And at Piglet's house he found Rabbit. So they all talked about it together.

"What I don't like about it is this," said Rabbit.

"Here are we—you, Pooh, and you, Piglet, and Me—and suddenly—"

"And Eeyore," said Pooh.

"And Eeyore—and then suddenly—"

"And Owl," said Pooh.

"And Owl—and then all of a sudden—"

"Oh, and Eeyore," said Pooh. "I was forgetting *him*."

"Here—we—are," said Rabbit very slowly and carefully, "all—of—us, and then, suddenly, we wake up one morning and, what do we find? We find a Strange Animal among us. An animal of whom we have never even heard before! An animal who carries her family about with her in her pocket! Suppose *I* carried *my* family about with me in *my* pocket, how many pockets should I want?"

"Sixteen," said Piglet.

"Seventeen, isn't it?" said Rabbit. "And one more for a handkerchief—that's eighteen. Eighteen pockets in one suit! I haven't time."

There was a long and thoughtful silence . . . and then Pooh, who had been frowning very hard for some minutes, said: "*I* make it fifteen."

"What?" said Rabbit.

"Fifteen."

"Fifteen what?"

"Your family."

"What about them?"

Pooh rubbed his nose and said that he thought Rabbit had been talking about his family.

"Did I?" said Rabbit carelessly.

"Yes, you said—"

"Never mind, Pooh," said Piglet impatiently.

"The question is, What are we to do about Kanga?"

"Oh, I see," said Pooh.

"The best way," said Rabbit, "would be this. The best way would be to steal Baby Roo and hide him, and then when Kanga says, 'Where's Baby Roo?' we say, *'Aha!'* "

"Aha!" said Pooh, practising. *"Aha! Aha!* ... Of course," he went on, "we could say 'Aha!' even if we hadn't stolen Baby Roo."

"Pooh," said Rabbit kindly, "you haven't any brain."

"I know," said Pooh humbly.

"We say *'Aha!'* so that Kanga knows that *we* know where Baby Roo is. *'Aha!'* means 'We'll tell you where Baby Roo is, if you promise to go away from the Forest and never come back.' Now don't talk while I think."

"That was what we decided at the time," said Pooh. "If we had to decide it now, I think we would decide differently, because Kanga is really very nice and not at all Strange."

"That is only because we have gotten to know Kanga," said Rabbit. "If you take the time to get to know someone, you usually find they are not so strange after all, even if they seem very different at first. But we are not talking about NOW. We are talking about THEN. At the time Kanga seemed like a Strange Animal that we would be better off not having in the Forest."

The Stranger had been listening carefully to all of

this because he had forgotten some things about the story.

"If I understand it correctly, then," he said, "the objective that you established was to get Kanga to leave the Forest and never come back."

"Yes," said Rabbit.

"Yesssss," said Pooh in an I'm-not-quite-sure tone of voice. "But we also decided to steal Baby Roo and hide him and not give him back unless Kanga left the Forest. Isn't that an objective?"

"Well, let's see," said The Stranger. "When a manager is setting objectives in her area of responsibility, those objectives should follow certain rules. Those rules tell us 'How' to set objectives that are valid and appropriate. If we review those rules, maybe we can decide what your objective really was and if you did a good job in establishing it."

"I like learning about the 'How,'" said Pooh. "'Hows' are difficult."

"The first rule for establishing objectives is that they must be derived from and be in accordance with the basic purpose or mission of the organization. In other words, you have to know what the organization was set up to do, what its business really is. Then you can design your objectives in any particular situation so they will make a contribution to accomplishing that purpose.

"Without a clear understanding of what the organization's mission is, there is no way a manager can decide what his objectives should be."

"Who decides what the purpose of an organization is?" asked Rabbit.

"That is one of the primary responsibilities of top management. Unfortunately, it also is one that is frequently neglected. Often everyone thinks that the answer is obvious. Usually it isn't, and determining it requires a lot of hard work and thinking. When top management hasn't established what the purpose is, the organization will almost always get into trouble.

"A good example of this is railroads in the United States. Everyone connected with them knew that their business was 'railroading.' Actually, the purpose of their business was to move or transport things from one place to another. They concentrated on railroading while the trucking companies and airlines took away their business. By not establishing what their purpose or mission was, the railroads missed opportunities and came on hard times.

"They had confused the means, a railroad, with the ends—viable and appropriate transportation."

"I can understand that," said Pooh. "Maybe stealing Baby Roo was a means and not an objective."

"I think it may be too soon to decide until we know the other rules," said The Stranger. "Let's go on and cover those.

"The second rule comes from the fact that you can't

do an objective or a goal. The objective must be able to be translated into specific work and assignments that will be carried out to reach the goal.

"Next, the objective must concentrate on the really important things so that you make the best use of the resources available to you since no one and no organization has all the resources needed to do everything.

"Then you should always have multiple objectives, because in any endeavor you are trying to balance a variety of needs, and that requires more than one objective.

"Objectives must make sense. The questions you ask to determine this are: 'Is it reasonable?' and 'Can we do it?'

"If the answer you get is no, then you had better redraft your objectives. Few individuals will work very well to achieve something when they perceive that failure is preordained.

"Finally, objectives should not be cast in concrete, since they are based on a guess about the future—ideally, an informed guess, but still a guess. Since the future holds many surprises and many conditions are beyond our control, objectives should recognize this fact and contain an allowance for it."

"It seems to me," said Rabbit slowly, "that we didn't do badly in setting our objectives according to the rules except we should have paid more attention to the purpose of our organization before we set our objectives.

Then we should have had more of an allowance for things not going as we expected."

"Why is that?" asked The Stranger.

"I know," said Pooh. "If we had spent more time talking about our purpose, we might have seen that we felt that Kanga and Baby Roo coming to the Forest was possibly a threat to us. The purpose of our organization then would be to see if it really was a threat, and if so, what we should do about it."

"We just hopped to a conclusion," said Rabbit, "that Kanga was a threat, so that limited us in choosing our objectives."

"That's the trouble with not knowing what the real purpose or mission of an organization is," said The Stranger.

"Yes," said Pooh. "We could have had an objective of finding out if Kanga was a threat, say, by asking Christopher Robin."

"Or," added Rabbit, "by sending Piglet to say 'Hallo' to Kanga while Pooh and I watched to see if she ate him—"

"Which Piglet wouldn't have liked. But either plan would have been easier than what we did do," finished Pooh.

"What happened then?" asked The Stranger.

"Piglet had an objection," said Pooh, remembering.

"There's just one thing," said Piglet, fidgeting a bit. "I was talking to Christopher Robin, and he said that a

Kanga was Generally Regarded as One of the Fiercer Animals. I am not frightened of Fierce Animals in the ordinary way, but it is well known that, if One of the Fiercer Animals is Deprived of Its Young, it becomes as fierce as Two of the Fiercer Animals. In which case '*Aha!*' is perhaps a *foolish* thing to say."

"Piglet," said Rabbit, taking out a pencil, and licking the end of it, "you haven't any pluck."

"It is hard to be brave," said Piglet, sniffing slightly, "when you're only a Very Small Animal."

Rabbit, who had begun to write very busily, looked up and said:

"It is because you are a very small animal that you will be Useful in the adventure before us."

Piglet was so excited at the idea of being Useful that he forgot to be frightened any more, and when Rabbit went on to say that Kangas were only Fierce during the winter months, being at other times of an Affectionate Disposition, he could hardly sit still, he was so eager to begin being useful at once.

"What about me?" said Pooh sadly. "I suppose *I* shan't be useful?"

"Never mind, Pooh," said Piglet comfortingly. "Another time perhaps."

"Without Pooh," said Rabbit solemnly as he sharpened his pencil, "the adventure would be impossible."

"Oh!" said Piglet, and tried not to look disappointed. But Pooh went into a corner of the room and said proudly to himself, "Impossible without Me! *That* sort of Bear."

"Now listen all of you," said Rabbit when he had finished writing, and Pooh and Piglet sat listening very eagerly with their mouths open. This was what Rabbit read out:

PLAN TO CAPTURE BABY ROO

1. *General Remarks*. Kanga runs faster than any of Us, even Me.
2. *More General Remarks*. Kanga never takes her eye off Baby Roo, except when he's safely buttoned up in her pocket.
3. *Therefore*. If we are to capture Baby Roo, we must get a Long Start, because Kanga runs faster than any of Us, even Me. (*See* 1.)
4. A *Thought*. If Roo had jumped out of Kanga's pocket and Piglet had jumped in, Kanga wouldn't

know the difference, because Piglet is a Very Small Animal.

5. Like Roo.
6. But Kanga would have to be looking the other way first, so as not to see Piglet jumping in.
7. See 2.
8. *Another Thought.* But if Pooh was talking to her very excitedly, she *might* look the other way for a moment.
9. And then I could run away with Roo.
10. Quickly.
11. *And Kanga wouldn't discover the difference until Afterwards.*

"Then what did you do?" The Stranger asked Rabbit.

"I read it out and answered any questions they had. Then by going over it very carefully, I made certain that they each knew what it was they had to do. I also added into the plan any suggestions and ideas they had."

"I suggested that I tell Kanga a little bit of poetry," said Pooh proudly. "To distract her, you see, which was my part in the Plan."

"I think you did an excellent job of Organizing," said The Stranger.

"I did?" Rabbit sounded surprised. "Oh, yes. I did."

"When a manager organizes, he analyzes the activities and the decisions that are needed to meet the objectives. He develops a step-by-step plan and puts it in writing so that everyone connected with the endeavor can refer to it.

"The plan must tell when each step is to be done and who is responsible for doing it. He then classifies the work and divides it into manageable jobs. According to the requirements of those jobs, he selects individuals whose experience, talents, and abilities match those requirements and assigns them.

"Then he reviews the plan with the individuals, answers their objections, and incorporates their suggestions, when they are appropriate, into the plan.

"He then makes certain that each individual understands the plan and knows what they have to do.

"So, you can see, you did all of those things."

"Yes," said Rabbit. "Considering that we probably started with the wrong purpose, it was a good plan."

"And you did a good job of organizing," said Pooh.

"Thank you, Pooh," said Rabbit. "I couldn't have done it without you."

"I know," said Pooh modestly.

"My goodness," said The Stranger, looking at the sun and noticing that it was almost directly overhead. "It's time for lunch. Why don't we eat and you can tell me how it all came out."

So they opened up the picnic basket, spread a cloth in a nice shady spot, arranged all the food so that it was convenient to reach, and Rabbit began.

"We all went out to look for Kanga and Roo."

Kanga and Roo were spending a quiet afternoon in a sandy part of the Forest. Baby Roo was practising very small jumps in the sand, and falling down mouse-holes and climbing out of them, and Kanga was fidgeting about and saying, "Just one more jump, dear, and then we must go home." And at that moment who should come stumping up the hill but Pooh.

"Good afternoon, Kanga."

"Good afternoon, Pooh."

"Look at me jumping," squeaked Roo, and fell into another mouse-hole.

"Hallo, Roo, my little fellow!"

"We were just going home," said Kanga. "Good afternoon, Rabbit. Good afternoon, Piglet."

Rabbit and Piglet, who had now come up from the

other side of the hill, said, "Good afternoon," and "Hallo, Roo," and Roo asked them to look at him jumping, so they stayed and looked.

And Kanga looked too. . . .

"Oh, Kanga," said Pooh, after Rabbit had winked at him twice, "I don't know if you are interested in Poetry at all?"

"Hardly at all," said Kanga.

"Oh!" said Pooh.

"Roo, dear, just one more jump and then we must go home."

There was a short silence while Roo fell down another mouse-hole.

"Go on," said Rabbit in a loud whisper behind his paw.

"Talking of Poetry," said Pooh, "I made up a little piece as I was coming along. It went like this. Er—now let me see—"

"Fancy!" said Kanga. "Now Roo, dear—"

"You'll like this piece of poetry," said Rabbit.

"You'll love it," said Piglet.

"You must listen very carefully," said Rabbit.

"So as not to miss any of it," said Piglet.

"Oh, yes," said Kanga, but she still looked at Baby Roo.

"*How* did it go, Pooh?" said Rabbit.

Pooh gave a little cough and began.

LINES WRITTEN BY A BEAR
OF VERY LITTLE BRAIN

On Monday, when the sun is hot
I wonder to myself a lot:
"Now is it true, or is it not,

"That what is which and which is what?"
On Tuesday, when it hails and snows,
The feeling on me grows and grows
That hardly anybody knows
If those are these or these are those.

On Wednesday, when the sky is blue,
And I have nothing else to do,
I sometimes wonder if it's true
That who is what and what is who.

On Thursday, when it starts to freeze
And hoar-frost twinkles on the trees,
How very readily one sees
That these are whose—but whose are these?

On Friday—

"Yes, it is, isn't it?" said Kanga, not waiting to hear what happened on Friday. "Just one more jump, Roo, dear, and then we really *must* be going."

Rabbit gave Pooh a hurrying-up sort of nudge.

"Talking of Poetry," said Pooh quickly, "have you ever noticed that tree right over there?"

"Where?" said Kanga. "Now, Roo—"

"That was well done," said The Stranger. "If a manager finds a plan is not working, it should be changed as soon as possible."

"Thank you," said Pooh. "Go ahead Rabbit, read us the rest."

"Right over there," said Pooh, pointing behind Kanga's back.

"No," said Kanga. "Now jump in, Roo, dear, and we'll go home."

"You ought to look at that tree right over there," said Rabbit. "Shall I lift you in, Roo?" And he picked up Roo in his paws.

"I can see a bird in it from here," said Pooh. "Or is it a fish?"

"You ought to see that bird from here," said Rabbit. "Unless it's a fish."

"It isn't a fish, it's a bird," said Piglet.

"So it is," said Rabbit.

"Is it a starling or a blackbird?" said Pooh.

"That's the whole question," said Rabbit. "Is it a blackbird or a starling?"

And then at last Kanga did turn her head to look. And the moment that her head was turned, Rabbit said in a loud voice "In you go, Roo!" and in jumped Piglet into Kanga's pocket, and off scampered Rabbit, with Roo in his paws, as fast as he could.

"Why, where's Rabbit?" said Kanga, turning round again. "Are you all right, Roo, dear?"

Piglet made a squeaky Roo-noise from the bottom of Kanga's pocket.

"Rabbit had to go away," said Pooh. "I think he thought of something he had to go and see about suddenly."

"And Piglet?"

"I think Piglet thought of something at the same time. Suddenly."

"So then the plan worked perfectly," said The Stranger. "Well-l-l-l," said Pooh slowly. "Not exactly."

Of course as soon as Kanga unbuttoned her pocket, she saw what had happened. Just for a moment, she thought she was frightened, and then she knew she wasn't; for she felt quite sure that Christopher Robin would never let any harm happen to Roo. So she said to herself, "If they are having a joke with me, I will have a joke with them."

"Now then, Roo, dear," she said, as she took Piglet out of her pocket. "Bed-time."

"*Aha!*" said Piglet, as well as he could after his Terrifying Journey. But it wasn't a very good "*Aha!*" and Kanga didn't seem to understand what it meant.

"Bath first," said Kanga in a cheerful voice.

"*Aha!*" said Piglet again, looking round anxiously for the others. But the others weren't there. Rabbit was playing with Baby Roo in his own house, and feeling more fond of him every minute, and Pooh, who had decided to be a Kanga, was still at the sandy place on top of the Forest, practising jumps.

"I am not at all sure," said Kanga in a thoughtful voice, "that it wouldn't be a good idea to have a *cold* bath this evening. Would you like that, Roo, dear?"

Piglet, who had never been really fond of baths, shuddered a long indignant shudder, and said in as brave a voice as he could:

"Kanga, I see the time has come to spleak painly."

"Funny little Roo," said Kanga, as she got the bath-water ready.

"I am *not* Roo," said Piglet loudly. "I am Piglet!"

"Yes, dear, yes," said Kanga soothingly. "And imitating Piglet's voice too! So clever of him," she went on, as she took a large bar of yellow soap out of the cupboard. "What *will* he be doing next?"

"Can't you *see?*" shouted Piglet. "Haven't you got *eyes?* Look at me!"

"I *am* looking, Roo, dear," said Kanga rather severely. "And you know what I told you yesterday about making faces. If you go on making faces like Piglet's, you will grow up to *look* like Piglet—and *then* think how sorry you will be. Now then, into the bath, and don't let me have to speak to you about it again."

Before he knew where he was, Piglet was in the bath, and Kanga was scrubbing him firmly with a large lathery flannel.

"She also made him take some of Roo's Strengthening Medicine, which Piglet didn't like in the least, although Kanga told him it really was quite a nice taste when you got used to it." Pooh thought for a moment. "I'm really not quite sure that's true. At least I'm certain that I would never prefer it to honey. Still, I suppose it does make you strong. Look how far Kanga can jump."

"Then Christopher Robin came by and told Kanga that Roo was at my house playing," said Rabbit. "Actually, I became quite fond of him, and we are now great friends."

"And Christopher Robin had left the door open, and Piglet managed to escape and roll on the ground so that he got his own comfortable color back again," Pooh added.

"That was a very exciting adventure," said The Stranger. "Thank you for telling me how it came out."

And then he remembered that he had an appointment outside the Forest, so he quickly packed up his picnic basket and, telling Pooh he would see him tomorrow, left.

"Rabbit," said Pooh. "It seems to me that today is Tuesday."

"Yes," said Rabbit. "And if today is Tuesday, I'm supposed to be playing with Roo."

"And I'm supposed to meet Kanga for my weekly jumping lessons."

So they both hurried off in different directions.

On the way to the sandy place in the Forest, which was the best place to practice jumping, because if you fell down, you didn't hurt yourself, Pooh remembered that he had forgotten to sing his Manager Song for The Stranger.

"Bother," said Pooh. "Oh, well. I'll surely remember to sing it tomorrow—or maybe the next day."

IV

IN WHICH Piglet, Pooh, and Tigger Communicate After a Fashion, Learn the Rules, and Pooh Is a Very Forgetful Bear

"It has to be Wednesday," said Pooh.

"Why is that, Pooh?" asked Piglet.

"It just stands to reason. If yesterday was Tuesday, and tomorrow is Thursday, then today must be Wednesday."

Piglet thought about that for a moment. "Why does it have to be Wednesday?"

"Because, Piglet," explained Pooh patiently, "Wednesday always comes after Tuesday and before Thursday. So it comes in the middle."

"Not always," said Piglet.

"Always," said Pooh, being very firm.

"I remember last year it was Tuesday and then the next day was Christmas and the following day was Thursday," said Piglet, even more firmly. "I remember because it was a Particularly Fine Christmas. It had snowed very hard on Tuesday, the day before, which is how I remember it was Tuesday, and I had a Christmas tree which I had Very Carefully Decorated. When I got up on Christmas I found a large gift of haycorns under the tree, and a big red balloon that Christopher Robin had given me—"

"And a pot of honey, which I had given you."

"Which you ate all of, when you came around to wish me a Merry Christmas."

"Yes, I know. There's nothing like a good pot of honey on Christmas morning," said Pooh dreamily. "Or for that matter, anytime."

"But it was my gift, and you ate it all."

"It's the thought that counts," said Pooh.

"Oh," said Piglet. "That's true. I forgot. But, anyway, that proves it."

"Proves what?" asked Pooh, who was still thinking about honey.

"It proves that Wednesday doesn't always follow Tuesday. Sometimes Christmas comes the day after Tuesday."

"Oh," said Pooh. "I hadn't thought about that."

"Could today be Christmas?" Piglet was suddenly very worried because if it was, he was very far behind in his preparations.

"I . . . don't . . . think . . . so," said Pooh slowly. "Because on Christmas, in my experience, there is usually snow on the ground, and there isn't." He looked around very carefully to make sure that there wasn't a little patch of snow somewhere that he had missed. If there was a lit-

tle smidgen of snow just sort of lying around, then maybe it just might be a Christmas of Very Little Snowfall that had somehow crept up on them and he should run home to see if there was a large gift of honey waiting for him.

"No," said Piglet, also looking around, although he was thinking about haycorns. "There isn't."

"So, if it isn't Christmas, it must be Wednesday."

"I suppose so, but I'm not really sure." Piglet looked under the nearest bush to see if there might be snow there, and there wasn't so he looked all around. "Look, Pooh, there's Tigger coming. Why don't we ask him if today is Christmas or Wednesday?"

Tigger was Bouncing along pretending to hunt Whatever-It-Was that Tiggers hunted. Since he wasn't quite sure what "IT" was that Tiggers hunted, he was practicing on anything that he came upon. He would Bounce along until he saw something that looked likely and then he would get down very low to the ground and creep closer very carefully so as not to alert Whatever-It-Was.

When Piglet and Pooh came up to him, he was stalking a very large gorse-bush. "Hallo, Tigger," they said.

"Shhhhh," said Tigger very quietly. "I'm hunting a fierce Something-Or-Other. I'll be with you in just a minute." As Piglet and Pooh watched, Tigger slowly moved forward, keeping close to the ground, his tail twitching rapidly back and forth. Then with a loud *Worraworraworraworraworra* he jumped into the very middle of the gorse-bush, thrashed and rolled around, and, after a terrible struggle, managed to pull himself out, all covered with prickles.

"Have I won?" he asked cheerfully.

"That's just a harmless gorse-bush," said Pooh.

"If it's harmless, why did it bite me when I wasn't looking?"

"I don't think it did."

"Yes it did. It would have bitten me worse but I was too quick for it. See, I have bites all over."

"Those are just prickles," said Pooh. "You always get prickles if you happen to get into a gorse-bush."

"Maybe Tiggers don't hunt gorse-bushes." Tigger looked carefully at the gorse-bush so as to remember that it wasn't the Sort-Of-Thing that Tiggers hunted.

"I suspect not," said Pooh, as he and Piglet began to help Tigger get rid of the prickles. "They aren't even good to eat. The only one I know who might like to eat them would be Eeyore, who likes prickly things like Thistles." After they had gotten most of the prickles out of Tigger and he was feeling Bouncy again, Piglet, from behind Pooh, because he was a Very Small Animal and being Bounced on might seriously damage him, asked, "Tigger, is today Wednesday?"

"Or is it Christmas?" asked Pooh. Hoping that there still might be a small chance that it was.

Tigger considered this, first sitting down and then getting up rather quickly to remove a prickle that they had missed and then sitting down again.

"I think," he said at last, "that it can't be Christmas, because, if it were, we would all be over at Christopher Robin's house helping him open his presents like we do every year. So it must be Wednesday. Why do you want to know?"

"Because The Stranger said he would see me tomorrow and he isn't here." Pooh didn't have to explain about The Stranger because everyone in the Forest knew about him by now.

"Well, that explains it," said Tigger. "It's not tomorrow. It's today. You're a day early, Pooh."

"Not really," said Pooh. "Because he said it yesterday and yesterday's tomorrow is today and not tomorrow, just like tomorrow's yesterday would be today." He paused to make sure that he had gotten it right. "Which is Wednesday, you see, if it isn't Christmas, because yesterday I took jumping lessons from Kanga, which always happens on Tuesdays."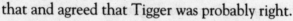

"If The Stranger is supposed to be here, and he isn't," said Tigger, looking around, "then he must be Someplace Else." Pooh and Piglet thought about that and agreed that Tigger was probably right.

"Maybe he's lost," squeaked Piglet.

"If that's so," said Pooh, remembering about Establishing Objectives and Organizing, "our objective should be to find him. Since there are three of us, we will all go in different directions because that way we will have a better chance to find him."

"If he is lost," said Piglet, trying to keep out of the way of Tigger by moving around Pooh, "instead of thinking that tomorrow is tomorrow. That is."

Pooh was too busy Organizing to listen. "Piglet, since you have the shortest legs, you will look at the closest Someplace Else, which would be around Rabbit's and Eeyore's houses. I'll go over and look in the Hundred Acre Wood, which is the next closest Someplace Else. Tigger, you look on the other side of the Forest near the bee-tree."

Then Pooh reviewed their assignments with them to make certain that each knew exactly where to go.

"After we have looked, we'll meet back here just before lunch." That was just in case The Stranger had brought his picnic basket with him.

So they all set off in their proper directions.

Pooh was the first to return because Piglet had found a Very Nice Patch of haycorns and that had delayed his search. When he saw Piglet coming along, munching on the last of the haycorns, he called out, "Did you find The Stranger?" thinking that perhaps carrying a Very Heavy picnic basket might have caused him to lag behind Piglet.

"No," said Piglet. "I did find a Very Nice Patch of haycorns, so it wasn't a complete waste. Did you?"

"I didn't find a single haycorn," said Pooh. "If I had I would have brought them back for you."

"I meant, did you find The Stranger?" Piglet looked all around to make certain The Stranger wasn't hiding behind a tree so that he could jump out and say "Surprise!" at Piglet. Piglet was a Very Small Animal and was not too fond of People jumping out unexpectedly.

"No," said Pooh. "Let's hope that Tigger found him." So they settled down to wait. Pooh kept glancing at the sun, which was almost overhead, although he really didn't have to since his stomach told him it was almost lunchtime.

After what seemed to be a long time, but really wasn't, Tigger came Bouncing along through the trees.

"Did you find The Stranger?" Pooh and Piglet called out together.

"Of course," answered Tigger. "Tiggers always find Strangers if they go looking for them."

"Where is he?" Pooh stretched up as tall as he could to see where The Stranger was, and if he had a heavy picnic basket with him.

"He's over on the other side of the Forest, near the bee-tree, sitting on a rock with his picnic basket beside him."

"Why didn't you bring him back with you?" asked Pooh.

"You didn't say to bring him back," said Tigger reproachfully. "You just said to find him. Which I did. And almost right away. I watched him for a long time, but he didn't do anything except sit there. I was behind a bush, so he didn't see me. Tiggers are very cunning about things like that, you know."

"Well, if you found him right away, why didn't you

come right back and tell us so we wouldn't waste our time looking Someplace Else when he wasn't there?"

Tigger shook his head. "You didn't say to find him and come right back. You said to find him and then we would meet here just before lunch. Which is now. I remember distinctly you said that."

"Bother! You misunderstood me," said Pooh.

"If you didn't mean what you said," Tigger pointed out logically, "then you should say what you mean."

"Well, there's no helping it now. We'll just have to go over to the bee-tree." Pooh shook his head sadly.

"Since it's lunchtime now, he probably will have eaten everything in his picnic basket by the time we get there. Oh, bother!"

Fortunately, he hadn't.

While they were eating lunch, which included some gourmet haycorns for Piglet, imported Extract of Malt for Tigger, and, of course, a large pot of honey for Pooh, The Stranger was told about the difficulties they had had in finding him.

"It seems to me as if there were problems with communication," he said. "In a way, that is fortunate, because that is one of the things we are going to talk about today."

"What's communication?" asked Piglet, who hadn't been with Pooh when it had been talked about.

"It means telling everyone working on a project what is happening. Everyone needs to communicate,

because that's how we learn and
live. From the information we receive, we make decisions about
what to do, what not to do, how to
work, how to live, how others are
relating to us, what they are
thinking and feeling, and what is important to them.

"From the information we give, others learn the
same things.

"Which is why communication is so important to a
manager. It is a manager's job to get things done, and the
only way that things get done is by an exchange of information. If a manager is not good at communicating, individuals will not understand what is wanted. They will not
know how to direct their efforts in trying to achieve the
objectives that have been set, and they will not know how
they are doing. Since others working with them will have
the same problem, there will be duplication of effort or,
even worse, some necessary things will not get done at all."

"Are there rules?" asked Pooh. "I like rules. Then I
know if I am doing things in the correct manner."

"Yes," answered The Stranger. "Suppose I tell you
the rules and then you can tell me why you had difficulties this morning."

"Do the rules apply to Tiggers?" asked Tigger.

"They apply to everyone who needs to exchange information, which, by the way, is another definition of
communication."

"Good!" Tigger sat up straighter. "Tiggers like to communicate."

"That's fortunate," said The Stranger. "If you like something, you will tend to be good at it."

"Tiggers are Very Good at communication," said Tigger in a very decided voice.

"The nice thing about communication is that almost anyone can improve her performance and become a better communicator."

"If she follows the rules," said Piglet.

"Yes. Which brings us to the first rule." The Stranger took a large tablet from his picnic basket and wrote down the first rule in big letters. When he had finished, he showed it to the others and read it aloud.

1. TO COMMUNICATE THERE MUST BE AN EXCHANGE OF INFORMATION.

"This rule says several things. There must be at least two individuals. There can be many individuals involved in the communication, but there must be at least two. Next there must be an exchange of information. That means that all communication should be a two-way process—back and forth, if you like, with all individuals who are participating both getting and giving information."

"Does that mean," asked Pooh, "that if I am telling

Tigger that he should search the other side of the Forest, I should be getting information from him also?"

"Absolutely. At the very least he should give you the information that he knows what he is to do and that he will do it."

"That's so I will know that I communicated properly."

"Exactly. The word for it is 'Feedback,' which we'll talk about after we've covered the other rules.

"Now the second rule is this:

2. ALL INFORMATION EXCHANGED SHOULD BE AS CLEAR AND COMPLETE AS POSSIBLE.

"There is a law called 'Murphy's Law' that states: 'If anything can be misunderstood, it will be misunderstood.' There are many reasons why we don't understand information that we receive. One reason is that the same word or words mean different things to different people."

"Like when Owl said, 'On the other hand—' and I thought he meant what he said, but what he really meant was 'As distinguished from,' " said Pooh.

"That's a good example," said The Stranger. "Let me give you another in the form of a little game."

"Good," squeaked Piglet. "I like games."

"I will say a word, and then you each tell me what that word meant to you. Ready? The word is 'house.' "

Tigger said, "Kanga's."

Piglet said, "Eeyore's."

Pooh said, "Owl's."

"We have three different meanings then for the one word 'house.' Why did you pick those words for your answer?"

"I live at Kanga's house," answered Tigger. "So I thought of her house."

"I was remembering when Pooh and I built a house for Eeyore," said Piglet. "It's the only house I ever built, so I thought of that."

"And I thought of Owl's because it is a Very Grand Indeed house, and I was just talking about Owl saying 'On the other hand,' which happened at his house." Pooh paused for a moment and then said, "Communication is very difficult if the same word means different things to different people."

"Did I win?" asked Tigger.

"Yes. You all had very reasonable answers," said The Stranger.

"Good," said Tigger. "I like to win games."

"You can see from this that if I asked you all to meet me at the house, it is very likely that we would all end up in a different place—just because the same word has different meanings to different people. So you must be careful with the words that you use."

"It seems to me that there must be other reasons," said Piglet. "Even when I use words that we all know, I sometimes have problems."

"Yes. Another very common reason that causes problems is that people don't always pay attention. This is particularly true with verbal communication. The problem is that we can think much faster than someone can talk, so our minds tend to wander, and we miss parts of the information even though we think we are listening carefully."

"I'm sorry," interrupted Pooh. "I didn't hear that last part. I was watching the bees in the bee-tree and thinking they must be making lots of honey because they are buzzing very loudly." So The Stranger repeated what he had said, and Pooh was a Very Embarrassed Bear. However, The Stranger said it was all right because it Proved the Point.

"Of course," The Stranger continued, "all of your information should be complete. The danger here is that, as a manager, you are so familiar with what you want to communicate, you might leave something out. So you need to review carefully everything you will be communicating to make certain it is complete."

"Like Pooh not saying that I was to bring you back," said Tigger. "When I found you, that is."

"Yes. That's a good example. Now we come to a very important rule that is often overlooked." The Stranger wrote it on his tablet.

3. THE INFORMATION SHOULD BE MEAN-INGFUL TO THE INDIVIDUAL WHO IS RECEIVING IT.

"There are really two reasons for this rule. The first is that even if the information is clear and complete, the individual who is receiving the information will not pay much attention to it unless it is meaningful, or you could say 'important,' to him. As the saying goes, 'It goes in one ear and out the other.'

"Now, you probably wouldn't be bothering to communicate the information unless you felt that it was important to those who were receiving it, so you must express it in a way that stresses what is important to them.

"For instance, if you are managing a factory and there is the need to increase production because you are not meeting delivery dates that your customers require, you could call your people together and tell them that. However, that probably isn't very meaningful to most of them, so they won't pay attention, or they won't take it very seriously, figuring that is the sales department's problem.

"On the other hand—"

"He means as distinguished from the first thing," Pooh whispered to Piglet.

"If you tell them that the customers may cancel their orders unless delivery is improved, and if that happens, there may have to be layoffs, you can be sure you will have their attention, because now the information is important to them.

"The second reason is that there is not much point in telling someone something that is not of importance to her. You are just wasting her time and yours."

"Sometimes Eeyore goes on at great length about the new Thistle patch he has found," said Pooh. "I am glad he found it, of course, but really, I am not all that interested in Thistles."

"What do you do when that happens?"

"I usually think about what I would do if I found a big pot of honey." Pooh shook his head. "Honey is much more difficult to find than Thistles. Then when I realize that Eeyore has stopped talking about Thistles, I pay attention again."

"You see, that is exactly what the rule guards against."

"Are there more rules?" asked Tigger. He was beginning to Bounce.

"There are two more, and they are Very Important." The Stranger wrote down the next rule in even bigger letters than he had before.

4. ALWAYS GET CONFIRMATION THAT THE MESSAGE YOU ARE COMMUNICATING HAS BEEN UNDERSTOOD.

"This is called 'feedback.' It means that because of all the reasons we have been talking about, you should always make certain that the message you were communicating was understood. You do this by asking those to whom you are giving the information to tell you what information they received and by listening Very, Very Carefully to what they tell you.

"If what they tell you is not correct, then you tell them what they have not understood or have missed, and you repeat this process until you are certain they have understood your message. You see, to be a good communicator, you must be a good listener."

"Tiggers are Very Good Listeners," said Tigger. "That's why I know that Pooh didn't say to bring you back when I found you."

"And I didn't ask for feedback from him," said Pooh. "That's where I

went wrong. I fear I am a Bear of Very Little Brain."

"But then you didn't know the rule," pointed out The Stranger.

"That's true," said Pooh. "I would do much better now."

"So now we come to the last rule."

5. INFORMATION CAN BE GIVEN IN MANY WAYS. THE MORE WAYS YOU USE, THE CLEARER AND MORE BELIEVABLE IT

**WILL BE. HOWEVER, THE MESSAGE
MUST BE THE SAME IN ALL WAYS. IT IS
VITAL TO BE CONSISTENT.**

Pooh, Piglet, and Tigger looked at the rule carefully.

"I ... don't ... understand ... it," Piglet said finally. "I thought if you had a message for someone, you just told them." Then he quickly added, "Making sure that it is clear, complete, and meaningful, of course."

"And getting feedback," Pooh added. "That's very important."

"Well," said The Stranger, "there are really many ways that we use to communicate and to get our messages across.

"We are using two right now. We are talking about the rules of communication. That's called giving information verbally—in other words, we hear the information. At the same time, I am writing it down on this tablet, so we can see it. That's called giving information visually—we see it.

"Then we could combine those two ways so that we give the information in two forms at the same time—as in a movie or a TV program. That's really a third way.

"The most important way, particularly for a manager, is information given by the way he acts. The individuals who are receiving the information will watch him closely to see if the way he acts gives the same message that he is giving by other ways such as verbally or visually. If his actions convey a message that is different from what he is saying or writing, they will assume that he really doesn't mean what he is saying or writing."

"I still don't understand," said Piglet, "about the acting part, that is, and giving information by what you do."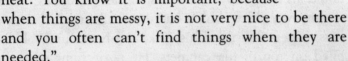

"Let's take an example, then. Suppose you are a manager, and you notice that the place where everyone works is not clean or neat. You know it is important, because when things are messy, it is not very nice to be there and you often can't find things when they are needed."

"I was clean once," interrupted Piglet. "Kanga gave me a bath when I was pretending to be Roo." He thought for a moment. "I didn't like it very much. Being clean, that is. It wasn't comfortable and it changed my color."

"We were talking about the place where everyone works," said Pooh. "Not about the ones who work there."

"Oh," said Piglet. "Excuse me. Please go on."

"So the manager calls everyone together and shows them how messy everything is, points out how much nicer it will be if it is clean and neat and how their work will be easier if the situation is changed. He then asks for their suggestions about what should be done and incorporates their ideas into his own plan. He organizes the work, writes it down, gives everyone a copy, posts it on the bulletin board, and gets feedback to make sure that it is understood."

"So then the place became clean and neat," said Tigger. "I like happy endings."

"Unfortunately, it didn't."

"I don't see why it didn't," said Pooh. "It seems to me that the manager followed all the rules."

"It didn't because the manager made a mistake that undid all the good work he had done. He didn't clean up his own office, which had dust balls in all the corners, papers falling off his desk, and books and folders piled on top of file cabinets. He also crumpled up a piece of paper when he was out in the shop where everyone was working and just threw it on the floor. So everyone decided from his actions that being clean and neat was not really very important and didn't do anything themselves."

"I see," said Piglet. "You could say that actions speak louder than words."

"That's very good, Piglet. I'll just add it to the last rule."

"It's original too," said Piglet proudly. "I just thought it up."

The Stranger wrote down what Piglet had said and added a title at the beginning so that what was written on the tablet looked like this:

RULES FOR EFFECTIVE COMMUNICATION

1. TO COMMUNICATE THERE MUST BE AN EXCHANGE OF INFORMATION.
2. ALL INFORMATION EXCHANGED SHOULD BE AS CLEAR AND COMPLETE AS POSSIBLE.
3. THE INFORMATION SHOULD BE MEANINGFUL TO THE INDIVIDUAL WHO IS RECEIVING IT.
4. ALWAYS GET CONFIRMATION THAT THE MESSAGE YOU ARE COMMUNICATING HAS BEEN UNDERSTOOD.
5. INFORMATION CAN BE GIVEN IN MANY WAYS. THE MORE WAYS YOU USE, THE CLEARER AND MORE BELIEVABLE IT WILL BE. HOWEVER, THE MESSAGE MUST BE THE SAME IN ALL WAYS. IT IS VITAL TO BE CONSISTENT. REMEMBER, ACTIONS SPEAK LOUDER THAN WORDS.

They all looked at the list written on the tablet.

"I can see why we had difficulty this morning," Pooh said at last. "We didn't follow the rule about information being as clear and complete as possible, and we didn't get feedback."

"Exactly," said The Stranger. "It was a good example of why the manager must be very careful when she is communicating and must think about it before she does it and while she is doing it. All managers should practice the rules until they become second nature."

"I'm not going to practice hunting now," said Tigger. "I'm going to find Eeyore and practice communication." With a loud *Worraworraworraworraworra* he Bounced off in the direction of Eeyore's house.

"Thank you," said Piglet to The Stranger. "I'm sure that things will be much clearer from now on. I think I'll go see Owl and find out if he can communicate to me where he might have seen a patch of haycorns recently." He started off toward the Hundred Acre Wood.

After Tigger and Piglet had left, The Stranger and Pooh agreed that they would meet the next day. They made very certain this time that they followed the rules of communication, and The Stranger complimented Pooh on his Particularly Excellent use of feedback.

It was only after The Stranger had left that Pooh realized that he hadn't sung his Manager Song. "I am a Very Forgetful Bear," he said to himself. "I forgot it again. Oh, bother!"

V

IN WHICH Pooh Finally Sings His
Manager Song, Eeyore Wanders By, an
Expotition Is Remembered, and
Motivation, Delegation, and Leadership
Are Explored

Pooh was a Very Determined Bear. Twice he had forgotten to sing his Manager Song to The Stranger.
This morning he would not forget because it was an
Important Song. It was Important because it was to
remind himself to ask The Stranger about words like
"leader" and "delegate," and how they fit into a manager's job.

The best way not to forget was to sing the song to
himself all the way from his house until he saw The
Stranger. So, as he walked along through the heather,
he sang the song to himself.

> *The manager, manager,*
> *A leader must be.*
> *That's Most Important,*
> *As we all can see.*

After he had sung it over and over, he tried humming it, but somehow it didn't make a very good Hum, so he went back to singing it. He went on singing it until he came to the part of the stream where the stepping-stones were, and when he was in the middle of the third stone, he began to wonder why the song did not

feel like a Good Song. So he sat down on the stone in the middle of the stream and thought about it.

The sun was so delightfully warm, and the stone, which had been sitting in it for a long time, was so warm too that Pooh almost forgot to think about the song, but then he remembered that he had to meet The Stranger and that the song should be a Good Song lest The Stranger would think that he didn't deserve to become a V.I.B.

"It seems to me," he said, "that since the song is about a Very Important Thing and is used to remind me about Very Important Words, it should be a Very Important Song."

He watched a dragonfly hover overhead while he thought about that. "Bother! The trouble is, it doesn't sound like a Very Important Song."

He sang it again, Just To Be Sure. The dragonfly darted away, which proved that it wasn't a Very Important Song, because if it had been, the dragonfly would surely have stayed to see how it came out.

"It seems to me," thought Pooh, "that if it is to be a Very Important Song, it should be longer." So he made up some more for the song.

> *He delegates work*
> *To those that he trusts.*
> *Objectives and organizing*
> *Are some of his musts.*

Pooh decided that the second verse made the song a more Important one, so he got up off his stone and went to meet The Stranger.

As he walked, he thought that if one more verse

made the song seem more Important, then a third verse might make it seem Very Important, which was what was wanted. So, as he walked, he wiped his mouth with the back of his paw to remove a little something left over from the little something of marmalade and honey he had had for breakfast and sang a rather fluffy third verse through the fur. It went like this:

> *He does all these things*
> *As well as he can.*
> *For they are all part*
> *Of a manager's plan.*

Written down like this, it doesn't seem like a Very Important Song, but coming through pale fawn fluff at about half-past nine on a very sunny morning, it seemed to Pooh to be one of the Most Important Songs he had ever sung. So he went on singing it all the way to where The Stranger was waiting for him.

"Hallo, Pooh," said The Stranger. "Did you make up that song?"

"Well, I sort of made it up," said Pooh. "It isn't Brain," he went on humbly, "because it just sort of comes to me, you know, so I can remember to ask you about what Owl said is important. Which is a manager being a leader and delegating."

"Those are important and it seems to me that your song is Very Appropriate. We were going to talk about motivation today. We can cover leadership and delegation at the same time."

"Oh," said Pooh. "Thank you. About the song, I mean." Pooh was not quite sure what "Appropriate" meant, but it sounded Important. He then told The Stranger all about his conversation with Owl or at least the part he had forgotten to tell him about last time.

"I am pretty certain about delegation," he finished, "but I'm not sure what a leader is, and why it is important that a manager should be a leader."

"Well," said The Stranger, "why don't we see if you can think of an adventure that had a leader, and we can see what that tells us about what a leader is."

"It's hard to think of an adventure that had a leader if one is not sure what a leader is," pointed out Pooh in a Very Reasonable tone of voice.

"That's a very good point. A leader is an individual who goes ahead and others follow."

"Oh," said Pooh. "That kind of an adventure. I remember—" but he had to stop because, just at that moment, Eeyore wandered into sight, saw Pooh and The Stranger talking, and came over to them.

"Hallo, Pooh," he said. "I found my tail just where you said. It was pretending to be a bell-pull, but it couldn't fool me." Eeyore looked back at his tail, which was following close behind him.

"That's a very fine tail," said The Stranger, and introduced himself.

"As tails go, I suppose it's all right," said Eeyore sadly. "Actually, tails are supposed to go where the individual who is attached to them goes, and this one doesn't. Not always. Sometimes it goes and becomes a bell-pull. It's just my luck to have a tail that wants to be a bell-pull." After a long silence he added, "How like a tail." He looked back to make sure it was still there.

"That reminds me," said Pooh. "We were just talking about a tale. The one where we all went on an Expotition to discover the North Pole and Christopher Robin was our leader."

"I remember that," Eeyore said gloomily. "It didn't end very well. Speaking of end, you will remember what happened to my tail in that adventure, won't you?"

"Of course," said Pooh. "But that happened later. I'll tell it from the beginning so The Stranger will understand it."

"Very well," said Eeyore. "Just so you don't forget. Some do, you know. Forget their promises, that is."

Pooh promised not to forget the part about Eeyore's tail and began at the beginning.

"It all began with me meeting Christopher Robin," said Pooh.

Christopher Robin was sitting outside his door, putting on his Big Boots. As soon as he saw the Big Boots, Pooh knew that an Adventure was going to happen, and he brushed the honey off his nose with the back of his paw, and spruced himself up as well as he could, so as to look Ready for Anything.

"Good-morning, Christopher Robin," he called out.

"Hallo, Pooh Bear. I can't get this boot on."

"That's bad," said Pooh.

"Do you think you could very kindly lean against me, 'cos I keep pulling so hard that I fall over backwards."

Pooh sat down, dug  his feet into the ground, and pushed hard against Christopher Robin's back, and Christopher Robin pushed hard against his, and pulled and pulled at his boot until he had got it on.

"A good leader involves others in his preparations," said The Stranger. "What did he tell you then?"

"Then he told me this," said Pooh.

"We are all going on an Expedition," said Christopher Robin, as he got up and brushed himself. "Thank you, Pooh."

"Going on an Expotition?" said Pooh eagerly. "I don't

think I've ever been on one of those. Where are we going
to on this Expotition?"

"Expedition, silly old Bear. It's got an 'x' in it."

"Oh!" said Pooh. "I know." But he didn't really.

"We're going to discover the North Pole."

"Oh!" said Pooh again. "What *is* the North Pole?" he
asked.

"It's just a thing you discover," said Christopher
Robin carelessly, not being quite sure himself.

"Oh! I see," said Pooh. "Are bears any good at discovering it?"

"Of course they are. And Rabbit and Kanga and all
of you. It's an Expedition. That's what an Expedition
means. A long line of everybody. . . .

"That sounded as if it would be exciting," Pooh said.

"A good leader will always try to make the project
that she wants worked on seem to be exciting," said The
Stranger. "That is really part of motivating individuals.
Everyone will try to do a better job when they feel that
the project is exciting and significant. By being part of
something that is important, individuals will feel that
they are important—and everyone likes to feel that way."

"I wasn't sure what a North Pole was," said Pooh,
"but Christopher Robin said it was a thing you discover
and that sounded important. He also said that bears
were good at discovering it."

"That's another thing that leaders do. They encourage and praise those who are working with them. We all

like to live up to what someone thinks about us if it is good, so we will try harder to make the project or the work successful. Motivating really means giving someone a reason to do good work. Feeling that a task is important and living up to the good opinion that someone we respect has of us are both very strong reasons to do a good job.

"What did Christopher Robin do then?" The Stranger asked.

"He said this."

"You'd better tell the others to get ready, while I see if my gun's all right. And we must all bring Provisions."

"Bring what?"

"Things to eat."

"Oh!" said Pooh happily. "I thought you said Provisions. I'll go and tell them." And he stumped off.

"So that was some more motivation for you to join in the Expedition."

"Yes," said Pooh dreamily. "I had a large pot of honey and—"

"What happened next?" asked Eeyore. "I wasn't there, you know. Not at the Beginning. I almost never am. I know what they say. Eeyore doesn't have to be in at the start. He'll come along anyway. Let Eeyore bring up the end." Eeyore sighed. "That's just the way things are. Sad but true."

"When Christopher Robin asked you to tell the

others to get ready," asked The Stranger, "what do you think he was doing?"

Pooh thought for a moment. "I . . . guess . . . he . . . was . . . delegating," he said slowly.

"Exactly. He was giving you a part of his responsibilities to carry out, so that he would have time to do other things. What did you do then?"

"Well, the first person I met was Rabbit, and I told him about the Expotition and what the purpose was and that we were to bring things to eat and that we were to meet at Christopher Robin's. Then I asked him to go tell Kanga, while I went to find Piglet."

"So you delegated part of your task to Rabbit."

"Yes," said Pooh proudly. "I guess I did. Delegate, that is. I can see why Owl said delegation is important. It made my job easier and it got done faster."

"That's why managers use delegation as a very important tool. It allows them to multiply their efforts. You also did it the right way. You told Rabbit the objective and the reasons for the assignment. You gave him an important task to do—many managers delegate only unimportant or minor tasks, which is unfair to those they manage.

"What is even better is that you didn't tell him how to do it. You let him decide how to accomplish the task. If a manager delegates in that way, it gives subordinates a chance to learn and develop their own skills and abilities—to grow by doing parts of the boss's job."

"He didn't do it exactly right," said Pooh. "He brought all of his friends-and-relations, and I only told him to bring Kanga."

"That's not bad. A manager has to learn that when she delegates, those she delegates to may make mistakes. In fact, they almost always will. That is an important part of anyone's development and growth. By making mistakes you learn how to do things right, and you are not afraid to try new things.

"Remember, good judgment is the result of experience, and experience is the result of bad judgment."

"Anyway," said Pooh, "it didn't matter. Rabbit said they could march at the end, after Eeyore."

"It mattered to me," said Eeyore. "I found it unsettling. "But nobody cared because just then Christopher Robin said to come on, and we all went off after him in the order we were in. I was at the end, but I wasn't at the end."

"But you said it was all right," said Pooh.

"Yes, but I also said Don't Blame Me."

"What happened then?" asked The Stranger.

"I made up a song as we walked along," said Pooh, "and I was singing my song to Piglet when suddenly—"

"Hush!" said Christopher Robin turning round to Pooh, "we're just coming to a Dangerous Place. . . ."

"Hush!" said Piglet to Kanga.

"Hush!" said Kanga to Owl, while Roo said "Hush!" several times to himself very quietly.

"Hush!" said Owl to Eeyore.

"*Hush!*" said Eeyore in a terrible voice to all Rabbit's friends-and-relations, and "Hush!" they said hastily to each other all down the line, until it got to the last one of all. And the last and smallest friend-and-relation was so upset to find that the whole Expotition was saying "Hush!" to *him*, that he buried himself head downwards in a crack in the ground, and stayed there for two days until the danger was over, and then went home in a great hurry, and lived quietly with his Aunt ever-afterwards. His name was Alexander Beetle.

They had come to a stream which twisted and tumbled between high rocky banks, and Christopher Robin saw at once how dangerous it was.

"It's just the place," he explained, "for an Ambush."

"Well, I wasn't sure what kind of a bush Christopher Robin had said, so I whispered to Piglet, 'What sort of bush? A gorse-bush?' "

"Owl heard and said that an Ambush was a sort of Surprise. I told him that so is a gorse-bush sometimes. Then Owl said that if people jump out at you suddenly, that's an Ambush, and I told him about the time that a gorse-bush had sprung at me suddenly one day when I fell out of a tree and that it had taken me six days to get all the prickles out of myself. Owl said that we were not talking about gorse-bushes, but I told him that I was."

"We got past the Dangerous Place without an Ambush," said Eeyore. "Now we are almost at the interesting place in the Expo—what we did."

They were climbing very cautiously up the stream now, going from rock to rock, and after they had gone a little way they came to a place where the banks widened out at each side, so that on each side of the water there was a level strip of grass on which they could sit down and rest. As soon as he saw this, Christopher Robin called "Halt!" and they all sat down and rested.

"I think," said Christopher Robin, "that we ought to eat all our Provisions now, so that we shan't have so much to carry."

"That shows that Christopher Robin was a good leader," The Stranger said. "A leader has a sincere interest and concern for the people he manages. One way he shows this is by making certain that their needs are taken care of and that he is concerned for their well-being."

"My need was not taken care of," said Eeyore. "As Usual. Nobody told me to bring along something. How like Them. Nobody even offered to share."

"I shared," said Pooh. "I had by accident sat down on a thistle, and I got up rather quickly so you could eat it. So you could eat it and for another  reason." Pooh rubbed his sitting down place as he remembered the thistle.

"Thank you again, Pooh," said Eeyore. "That was very kind of you to share. As I told you at the time, however, sitting on them doesn't do them any good. Takes all the life out of them. Everyone should remember that and take care not to sit on a thistle if they encounter one. They could call me and I would advise them as to proper behavior toward a thistle."

"I'll remember that," said The Stranger. "What happened next?"

"Well," said Pooh, "Christopher Robin was off talking to Rabbit about the North Pole being a pole because it wouldn't be called a pole if it wasn't. Piglet was lying on his back sleeping peacefully. Roo was washing his face and paws in the stream, while Kanga explained to everybody proudly that this was the first time he had ever washed his face himself. . . ."

"I was saying that I didn't hold with all this washing," said Eeyore. "This modern Behind-the-Ears nonsense. You can't tell what may happen. Bound to be unhealthy, I say. Look what did happen."

"What did happen?" The Stranger asked.

"Roo fell into the stream," said Pooh, "and was being swept downstream over a waterfall into the next pool."

"So much for washing," said Eeyore.

"Everybody was doing something to help," Pooh went on. "Piglet was jumping up and down and making 'Ooo, I say' noises; Owl was explaining that in a case of Sudden and Temporary Immersion, the Important Thing was to keep the Head above Water; Kanga was jumping along the bank, saying 'Are you sure you're all right, Roo dear?' Roo was answering, 'Look at me swimming!' "

"This is the important part," said Eeyore. "I didn't lose my head. I turned around so that I wouldn't be distracted and hung my tail into the pool where Roo had fallen. I told him to catch onto it and he'd be all right."

"That was very quick thinking," said The Stranger.

"Yes," said Eeyore modestly. "I thought so at the time."

"But by that time, Roo had been swept two pools farther down the stream," said Pooh.

"I couldn't have known that," said Eeyore. "After all, I had my back to everything. It is very difficult, in case you've never noticed, to hang your tail in a pool while you are facing it."

"I suppose that's true," said Pooh. "Anyway, I went down two pools below where Roo was and found a long pole, and Kanga came up and took one end of it. We held it across the lower part of the pool, and Roo drifted up against it and climbed out."

"So Roo was rescued," said The Stranger.

"Yes, and something else happened. Christopher Robin came up and asked me where I had found the pole. I told him that I just found it. I thought it ought to be useful so I just picked it up."

"Pooh," said Christopher Robin solemnly, "the Expedition is over. You have found the North Pole!"

"That is all very nice," said Eeyore, "but I was sitting with my tail in the water."

Eeyore took his tail out of the water, and swished it from side to side.

"As I expected," he said. "Lost all feeling. Numbed it. That's what it's done. Numbed it. Well, as long as nobody minds, I suppose it's all right."

"Poor old Eeyore. I'll dry it for you," said Christopher Robin, and he took out his handkerchief and rubbed it up.

"Thank you, Christopher Robin. You're the only one who seems to understand about tails. They don't think— that's what's the matter with some of these others. They've no imagination. A tail isn't a tail to *them*, it's just a Little Bit Extra at the back."

"Never mind, Eeyore," said Christopher Robin, rubbing his hardest. "Is *that* better?"

"It's feeling more like a tail perhaps. It Belongs again, if you know what I mean."

"That's another characteristic of a leader," said The Stranger. "He treats individuals as individuals. He doesn't treat those with tails the same as he does those without tails. What else happened?"

They stuck the pole in the ground, and Christopher Robin tied a message on to it.

NORTH POLE
DISCOVERED BY POOH
POOH FOUND IT.

"That was very nice of Christopher Robin to do that," said The Stranger after admiring the message. "You see, Pooh, that is another thing that a good leader does. He gives credit to others. Since he was the leader of the Expedition, he could have said that he discovered the North Pole. Our natural tendency is to make ourselves look good. An effective leader's goal is to make his *people* look good."

"It made me feel proud of what I had done," said Pooh. "It made me feel so good I went home and had a little something to revive myself." Pooh looked at the picnic basket again, and this time The Stranger noticed.

As he unpacked the picnic basket, The Stranger continued talking. "I would say that Christopher Robin was a very good leader. First, he created an air of excitement about the job that was to be done. Then he kept the objective as simple as possible so that everyone could understand what needed to be done."

"Even Piglet," said Pooh, watching the basket being unpacked.

"Even Piglet," The Stranger agreed. "He acted as a role model—showing by his actions how he expected others to act. He treated individuals as individuals—with dignity and respect—and showed he was concerned with their welfare. When something happened like Roo falling in the stream, he stood out of the way and let the others get on with their job, not interfering unless he was really needed, because a leader's job is to lead, not to do. Finally, he gave credit to you, when he could have taken it himself."

"Yes," said Pooh. "I didn't know it was the North

Pole when I picked it up. Christopher Robin recognized it so he could have properly said that he discovered it and taken the credit."

"But he didn't, which shows he was a good leader."

Pooh didn't answer because he was too involved with a particularly good jar of honey, which tasted like the bees had made it from apple blossoms, but he nodded to show that he thought Christopher Robin was a Very Good Leader indeed.

VI

IN WHICH We Talk About Measuring
Ents, a Woozle Is Tracked to Its Lair and
Defined, and Pooh Gets to Know How
Much Honey He Has

Pooh was sitting in his house counting his pots of honey.

Waking up early that morning, just as the sun came in through the window and made interesting patterns on the floor, the Thought Had Occurred that it had been several days since The Stranger with his picnic basket had been in the Forest.

Once the Thought Had Occurred, another thought came right along behind it. If The Stranger hadn't come to the Forest in several days, he might not come with his picnic basket for several more days.

Pooh sat up in bed and watched the dust motes dance in the sunbeams. It seemed to him that the two thoughts were Significant. "Perhaps," he said to himself, "if I had a little something, All Would become Clear." So he got out of bed, selected a pot of honey from his honey-cupboard, and sat down at the table to think about the Thoughts.

As everyone knows, it is very difficult to think about Significant Thoughts when one is eating honey. So it was not until he had finished the pot of honey and was looking inside to see if just possibly a Little More might have been hidden away in a corner that he realized why the Thoughts were Significant.

If The Stranger hadn't come to the Forest for several days, he might not come for several days more, and if he didn't come he wouldn't be bringing his picnic basket, and that was Significant. Without the picnic basket there wouldn't be any more extra pots of honey, and he, Pooh, would have to depend upon his own supply. The Thing to Do was to count how many pots he had in his honey-cupboard.

Pooh did this from time to time, anyway, even when there was no really good reason to do so, just because it was sort of comforting to be able to say to himself "I've got fifteen pots of honey left. Or sixteen, as the case may be."

He had found from experience that it was not nearly so comforting to say "I've got one pot of honey left," and to say "I've got no pots of honey left" was distinctly Uncomforting and Upsetting, so he usually waited to count until his larder was full.

This particular day, his larder was Very Full because The Stranger had brought so many pots of honey on his visits and had so nicely offered to share, even suggesting that Pooh take leftovers home, that Pooh had not used much of his own honey.

When the honey-cupboard was not full, Pooh could count the pots while they were in the cupboard because he kept them all on the bottom shelf where they were Easy to Reach.

When it was full, counting was a much more difficult task. He could never remember whether one counted the pots on one shelf and multiplied by three, or counted what was on each shelf and then added them all together. Since Pooh was really only sure of Times Twos, he usually decided to add, and even that was difficult since he was never sure if eleven added to six was eleventy-six or fourteen.

The best way, when the honey-cupboard was full, was to take all the pots out and put them in a line on the floor.

So he got a chair to stand on and began to move the pots from the cupboard to the floor.

When he had them all nicely arranged in an almost straight line, he began to count. He did very well until he came to the next to the last pot in the line. It was not a full pot. Pooh could look in and see that there was honey in it about halfway up.

"Bother," he said. "If it is a half-full pot, I should count it as half full. If it is half empty, I should count it that way." He finally decided that if he ate the honey, there would be no question. The pot would definitely be empty. So he did and it was.

He was just finishing counting when there came a knock on his door.

"Fourteen," said Pooh. "Come in. Fourteen. Or was it fifteen? Bother! That's muddled me."

"Hallo, Pooh," said The Stranger.

"Hallo. Fourteen, wasn't it?"

"What was?"

"My pots of honey that I was counting."

"Well," said The Stranger, "I heard you saying fifteen when I opened the door—just before you said 'Bother.' "

"Oh," said Pooh. "I guess I did. Now I shall have to count them again."

"Before you do that, why don't you add the three pots of honey I brought along? They are imported: one from France, one from Spain, and one from Italy. I would appreciate the opinion of an expert like you on which is best."

"Thank you very kindly," said Pooh. "The honey I like best comes from bees, but I shall be pleased to help out." And he added the three pots to those that were already on the floor. Since the pots already stretched from wall to wall, he had to start another line. He looked at them and scratched his head.

"Counting is difficult," he said to The Stranger, "unless you have them in a straight line. Even when they are all in a line, it is sometimes hard because all the pots are not the same size, and the question is if you should count two small pots as one big pot."

"I can see how that would be," said The Stranger.

"The thing is, it is more comforting to say that you have sixteen pots of honey, if you count two small ones separately, than if you say you have fifteen pots. But when it comes time to eat them, a small pot is Hardly Enough, so you end up eating two small ones, so it is just like you only had fifteen instead of sixteen."

"So you might as well count the two small ones as one."

"I suppose so." Pooh sighed. "It is comforting though to have an Extra Pot. Just for emergencies, you know, like a snowstorm or a flood when you can't get out to get more."

"An extra pot is comforting," The Stranger agreed.

"Then I had a problem of what to do about a pot that wasn't full and it wasn't empty, but I solved that."

"That's good."

"Yes, it was," said Pooh dreamily, licking his lips.

"It's not really surprising that you find counting difficult," said The Stranger. "Counting is measurement, which, as you remember, is part of a manager's job, and is usually the part that is done the least well by many managers."

"I can understand why," said Pooh, "but I thought it was measuring Ents."

"No, it was measurement. Remember, you stepped on the 'm' and scuffed it out so it looked like it was 'Measure ent.'"

"I am a bear of Very Little Brain. I forgot! But why does a manager bother with measurement? I know you told me, but I forgot that too."

"After a manager has set the objectives for what needs to be accomplished, organized the effort, and motivated the individuals who will be working, she needs to have a way to know what is happening and what progress is being made toward the established objectives. She gets this information by setting up yardsticks or measurements."

"Oh, yes," said Pooh. "Now I remember. Unless people know how they are doing, and what they are doing right, they can't improve their performance, or know if they are making progress toward achieving their objectives. As Eeyore would say, 'They won't know if they are reaching their goal or playing "Here we go gathering Nuts in May" with the end part of an ant's nest.'"

The Stranger smiled. "That's a very good way of describing the way things are if you don't have good measurements. So, a manager will see that everyone concerned has measurements available that not only show how the organization is performing but that also relate directly to the work of each individual.

"You see, Pooh, the manager interprets and analyzes the measurements, shows how they evaluate performance, and communicates this information to everyone—her subordinates, peers, and superiors. Basically, the manager sees that information is available that allows everyone to track the progress that is being made."

Pooh thought for a moment. "Piglet and I tracked something once."

"Why don't you tell me about it, and perhaps it will make this business of measurement clearer."

"Very well," said Pooh, settling down in his most comfortable chair, "although I'm not sure it will. Help, that is. The way it went was like this."

One fine winter's day when Piglet was brushing away the snow in front of his house, he happened to look up, and there was Winnie-the-Pooh. Pooh was walking round and round in a circle, thinking of something else, and when Piglet called to him, he just went on walking.

"Hallo! said Piglet, "what are *you* doing?"

"Hunting," said Pooh.

"Hunting what?"

"Tracking something," said Winnie-the-Pooh very mysteriously.

"Tracking what?" said Piglet, coming closer.

"That's just what I ask myself. I ask myself, What?"

"What do you think you'll answer?"

"I shall have to wait until I catch up with it," said Winnie-the-Pooh. "Now, look there." He pointed to the ground in front of him. "What do you see there?"

"Tracks," said Piglet. "Paw-marks." He gave a little squeak of excitement. "Oh, Pooh! Do you think it's a—a—a Woozle?"

"It may be," said Pooh. "Sometimes it is, and sometimes it isn't. You never can tell with paw-marks."

With these few words he went on tracking, and Piglet, after watching him for a minute or two, ran after him. Winnie-the-Pooh had come to a sudden stop, and was bending over the tracks in a puzzled sort of way.

"What's the matter?" asked Piglet.

"It's a very funny thing," said Bear, "but there seem to be *two* animals now. This—whatever-it-was—has been joined by another—whatever-it-is—and the two of them are now proceeding in company. . . ."

There was a small spinney of larch trees just here, and it seemed as if the two Woozles, if that is what they were, had been going round this spinney; so round this spinney went Pooh and Piglet after them. . . .

Suddenly Winnie-the-Pooh stopped and pointed excitedly in front of him. *"Look!"*

"What?" said Piglet, with a jump. And then, to show that he hadn't been frightened, he jumped up and down once or twice in an exercising sort of way.

"The tracks!" said Pooh. "*A third animal has joined the other two!*"

"Pooh!" cried Piglet. "Do you think it is another Woozle?"

"No," said Pooh, "because it makes different marks. It is either Two Woozles and one, as it might be, Wizzle, or Two, as it might be, Wizzles and one, if so it is, Woozle. Let us continue to follow them."

So they went on, feeling just a little anxious now, in case the three animals in front of them were of Hostile Intent. . . . And then, all of a sudden, Winnie-the-Pooh stopped again, and licked the tip of his nose in a cooling manner, for he was feeling more hot and anxious than ever in his life before. *There were four animals in front of them!* . . .

"I *think*," said Piglet, when he had licked the tip of his nose too, and found that it brought very little comfort, "I *think* that I have just remembered something. I have just remembered something that I forgot to do yesterday and shan't be able to do tomorrow. So I suppose I really ought to go back and do it now."

"So you were left to track the Woozles by yourself," said The Stranger.

"Not really," said Pooh.

Pooh looked up at the sky, and then, as he heard the whistle again, he looked up into the branches of a big oak-tree, and then he saw a friend of his.

"It's Christopher Robin," he said. . . .

Christopher Robin came slowly down his tree.

"Silly old Bear," he said, "what *were* you doing? First you went round the spinney twice by yourself, and then Piglet ran after you and you went round again together, and then you were just going round a fourth time—"

"Wait a moment," said Winnie-the-Pooh, holding up his paw.

He sat down and thought, in the most thoughtful way he could think. Then he fitted his paw into one of the Tracks . . . and then he scratched his nose twice, and stood up.

"Yes," said Winnie-the-Pooh.

"I see now," said Winnie-the-Pooh.

"I have been Foolish and Deluded," said he, "and I am a Bear of No Brain at All."

"You're the Best Bear in All the World," said Christopher Robin soothingly.

"It seems to me that it was a reasonable mistake to make," said The Stranger.

"Really?" said Pooh, brightening up. "But anyway, that was the end of the tracking story. Does it help—with measurement, that is?"

"It certainly does. It supplies me with just the word that I need to describe much of the information many managers and workers receive.

"You see, Pooh, the first thing a manager should ask when considering measurement is: What information do I, and the others who are concerned, need to do our jobs effectively? It should be measurements and information that will enable us to direct our efforts toward desired results that we can control."

"I can see that," said Pooh. "If your job was to fill pots with honey, it wouldn't do you any good to get information that told you how many Ents you should put in each pot."

"Exactly. Yet in many organizations the measurements and information that the manager receives is similar to that. It is like you and Piglet tracking the Woozle. The information you were receiving from the paw-marks led you around in a circle and didn't really mean anything. We could call information that does that 'Woozle Measurements,' in honor of your adventure."

Pooh said "Woozle Measurements" to himself several times, just to remind himself that it was named in honor of one of his adventures. He rather liked the sound of it. Certainly having something named in honor of one of your adventures could mean you were on the verge of becoming a Very Important Bear.

"The manager must make certain that the measurements she establishes are meaningful. They must measure and provide information on what she and others really need to know. They must not be 'Woozle Measurements.'

"For instance, in many plants a manager of a department may receive the quality control results or the production figures for the plant as a whole. The workers whom she supervises get nothing. What they really need is to receive figures or measurements that show what is happening in quality and production in the manager's area of responsibility."

"Why do managers get Woozle Measurements?" asked Pooh.

"Often simply because certain measurements are already being collected, and the manager accepts that because that is the way it has always been. Often the measurements have been set up by the accounting department, for accounting department needs, which may, and usually are, very different from what a manager and her people need to know. When she asks for something different, she is often told that the figures supplied were good enough for her predecessor, so they should be good enough for her, or that the computer or the system won't allow it, or that the figures and measurements are too expensive to collect just for her.

"The manager must not accept this. She must ask herself, 'What kind of information do I and the people I am responsible for and to really need to receive in order to do our jobs properly?' Once she has decided this, then she can work out how and where to get it and what form it should be in."

"But suppose the accounting department still won't give it to her?" asked Pooh.

"Often, if you really try, you can convince them, but if not, as a last resort, the manager can collect the information herself. After all, she can't do a proper job without it. She must have it to do an excellent job, as must her people. It is not fair to them or to herself to let it slide because it is difficult to get."

"I see," said Pooh. "Are there any other rules about measurements? I like rules. They are comforting."

"Well," said The Stranger, "they should be as economical to collect as is practicable. They should be kept as simple as possible. With data processing and computers it is tempting to generate masses and masses of figures. The information may be in there somewhere in the reports, but people won't take the time to dig it out. A good principle to follow is to use exceptions. Show measurements only when they deviate from what is expected. That way you don't waste time looking at measurements that are perfectly satisfactory, and those figures that require action stand out. Charts and graphs help also.

"In addition, measurements should be timely. If you need to know something today in order to take action, it doesn't do you much good to get the measurements about it next week, when it is too late. Finally, there is the most important rule of all about measurement."

"What is that?" asked Pooh, sitting up very straight as if he were getting ready to remember it.

"Measurements must be set up by the manager so that they are used to make self-control possible. If they are used—or, I should say, abused—to control people and to dominate them, there will be a great loss of effectiveness. This is a very common situation and one that managers, if they want to be excellent managers, must guard against. It is actually the main reason why measurement is the weakest part of most managers' performance."

"I'll remember that," said Pooh, "and I think I understand better about the 'How' of measurement. Could we try measuring my honey to see if I do it properly?"

"I think that would be a very good idea," said The Stranger.

Pooh said he thought what he really needed to know was how many pots of honey he should have in his honey-cupboard to be sure to get more before he ran out. That was seven, since he liked to have a pot of honey each day, and he had always been able to get more honey within a week.

Then he counted the pots he had and got the number exactly right, which was eighteen, counting the two

small pots as one and including the three that The Stranger had brought.

He put the seven pots on the top shelf, explaining

to The Stranger that when he had used everything on the bottom two shelves, he would know it was time to go and look for some more honey.

The Stranger said he thought that was a very fine control system, which is, of course, what measurement should be used for. "There is no point in having any measurements or reports or data, unless some action is taken based on them."

"Thank you," said Pooh. "It does seem like a good system. It is ever so much less Confusing, now that I know about measurement. And since now I've got the honey properly measured and put away, can I help you to bring your picnic basket over to the table?"

VII

IN WHICH Pooh, Owl, and The Stranger
Discuss the Others in the Forest to
Learn About Developing People and
Tiger is UnBounced

"It seems to me," said Pooh, "that there are two parts to it."

"Indisputably that is the case," said Owl. "Even a casual observation would reveal that there is indubitably an initial statement and then a final phrase."

"Oh," said Pooh. "I thought there were two parts to it."

"That," said Owl with dignity, "is what I said."

"I see," said Pooh. "I guess Indisputooly confused me."

Pooh had invited Owl over to his house to talk with The Stranger about the fourth function in a manager's work, that of developing people. Pooh felt that he knew less about that part of a manager's work than anything else a manager was supposed to do, and perhaps Owl's being there would help.

Owl had flown over from the Hundred Acre Wood just in time for breakfast, since he really preferred flying when the sun was not too bright. Knowing that, Pooh

had prepared for his visit by having on hand some of Owl's favorite breakfast food.

After they had finished eating,
and while they were waiting for
The Stranger, Pooh told Owl
about developing people.

"The Stranger said that a good
manager systematically works on
helping his people grow and improve and on improving
himself and his performance as a manager."

Owl nodded wisely, as if he had known that all
along, although he hadn't. Not really.

They had just decided that there were two parts to
the fourth function of a manager when Pooh's bell rang
and The Stranger came in. Owl had never met The
Stranger, so Pooh introduced them very nicely, as he
had been taught by Christopher Robin, who was learning about something called "Manners," which meant
helping elders and please and thank you and, of course,
doing introductions properly.

"I'm very pleased that you were able to come today,"
The Stranger said to Owl. "I was very impressed with
your grasp of management theories that Pooh told me
about. I'm sure you will add to today's discussion."

"Thank you," said Owl. "One does one's best, but
here in the Forest, one's opportunities for intelligent dis-
cussions about matters of moment tend to be somewhat

limited." Owl shook his head sadly from side to side. This was most impressive, since as Owl could turn his head almost all the way around, he appeared to be looking first over his right shoulder and then over his left shoulder.

"We already decided that developing people had two parts to it," said Pooh. "Owl said 'Indisputooly' that was so."

"The word," said Owl firmly, "was 'indisputably.'"

"Oh," said Pooh. "I forgot. I sometimes have difficulty with long words, although not with words like 'confuzzled' and 'expotition.'" Pooh wrinkled up his nose and scratched his head. "On the whole, I have less trouble with long 'X' words. Somehow they are easier to remember."

"If I had known that," said Owl, "I would have used an 'X' word instead. I could have said, 'Extenuating circumstances are lacking in this case.'"

"You're exactly right that there are two parts to the fourth function of a manager's job," said The Stranger. "I think we should talk about them separately."

"So we don't get Muddled," Pooh said.

"Yes. Although the objective is the same, the way a manager goes about developing his people is quite different from the way he improves himself and his performance as a manager."

"I think," said Owl, "that, if we are to have an intelligent discussion, we should say what the objective is in developing people."

"An excellent point. The objective should be to enable the individual to develop her talents and abilities to the fullest so that she can be effective in her work with the organization. Ideally, the objective is to achieve excellence within the limits of those talents and abilities and in accord with the individual's wishes."

"I see," said Owl. "Why don't we start with what the manager does to develop his people? That would be useful to know. For instance, there are some individuals here in the Forest that I think could stand some developing." And Owl named those he felt could stand some developing.

The Stranger chuckled. "I'm afraid what you have in mind, Owl, is not what we're talking about here. A manager does not try to make people over, or to change their basic personality. In the first place, I don't think that we know enough about people to be able to do that. Second, it would be deeply resented because it is manipulative and, I think, immoral."

"Still, some might profit from the process," said Owl.

"That's possible, but if we could in some way change the personality, then the individual would not be the same person. For instance, how would you describe Eeyore?"

"Eeyore is a quadruped of the horse kind but smaller, with long ears and a tuft at the end of the tail, who exhibits psychological manifestations of depression, pessimism, and occasional symptoms of a latent paranoid neurosis," said Owl.

"Eeyore is a donkey who is mostly gloomy and sad," said Pooh, "and who thinks 'They' take advantage of him and cause him problems."

"That, Pooh, is what I said," said Owl sternly.

"Oh," said Pooh. "Anyway, Eeyore is just Eeyore."

"Suppose for just a moment," said The Stranger, "that we could change Eeyore and make him like, say, Tigger, who is Bouncy and optimistic. What would you think about that?"

"You would have someone who looked like Eeyore and acted like Tigger," said Owl.

"But it wouldn't be Eeyore," said Pooh slowly. "I don't think I'd like it, and besides, one Bouncy Tigger is enough for a forest of this size. In fact," he continued, "sometimes it's almost too much. We even tried to un-Bounce Tigger once."

"Really," said The Stranger. "What happened?"

"It went something like this," said Pooh, remembering.

One day Rabbit and Piglet were sitting outside Pooh's front door listening to Rabbit, and Pooh was sitting with them. It was a drowsy summer afternoon, and the Forest was full of gentle sounds, which all seemed to be saying to Pooh, "Don't listen to Rabbit, listen to me." So he got into a comfortable position for not listening to Rabbit, and from time to time he opened his eyes to say "Ah!" and then closed them again to say "True," and from time to time Rabbit said, "You see what I mean,

Piglet," very earnestly, and Piglet nodded earnestly to show that he did.

"In fact," said Rabbit, coming to the end of it at last, "Tigger's getting so Bouncy nowadays that it's time we taught him a lesson. Don't you think so, Piglet?"

Piglet said that Tigger *was* very Bouncy, and that if they could think of a way of unbouncing him, it would be a Very Good Idea. . . .

"Well, I've got an idea," said Rabbit, "and here it is. We take Tigger for a long explore, somewhere where he's never been, and we lose him there, and next morning we find him again, and—mark my words—he'll be a different Tigger altogether."

"Why?" said Pooh.

"Because he'll be a Humble Tigger. Because he'll be a Sad Tigger, a Melancholy Tigger, a Small and Sorry Tigger, and Oh-Rabbit-I-*am*-glad-to-see-you Tigger. That's why."

"Will he be glad to see me and Piglet, too?"

"Of course."

"That's good," said Pooh.

"I should hate him to go *on* being Sad," said Piglet doubtfully.

"Tiggers never go on being Sad," explained Rabbit. "They get over it with Astonishing Rapidity. I asked Owl, just to make sure, and he said that that's what they always get over it with. But if we can make Tigger feel Small and Sad just for five minutes, we shall have done a good deed."

"Did you decide to go ahead with Rabbit's plan to change Tigger?" asked The Stranger.

"Yes, the very next day."

The next day was quite a different day. Instead of being hot and sunny, it was cold and misty. Pooh didn't mind for himself, but when he thought of all the honey the bees wouldn't be making, a cold and misty day always made him feel sorry for them. He said so to Piglet when Piglet came to fetch him, and Piglet said that he wasn't thinking of that so much, but of how cold and miserable it would be being lost all day and night on the top of the Forest. But when he and Pooh had got to Rabbit's house, Rabbit said it was just the day for them, because Tigger always bounced on ahead of everybody, and as soon as he got out of sight, they would hurry away in the other direction, and he would never see them again.

"Not never?" said Piglet.

"Well, not until we find him again, Piglet. Tomorrow, or whenever it is. Come on. He's waiting for us. . . ."

So they went. At first Pooh and Rabbit and Piglet walked together, and Tigger ran round them in circles, and then, when the path got narrower, Rabbit, Piglet and Pooh walked one after another, and Tigger ran round them in oblongs, and by-and-by, when the gorse got very prickly on each side of the path, Tigger ran up and down in front of them, and sometimes he bounced into Rabbit and sometimes he didn't. And as they got higher, the mist got thicker, so that Tigger kept disappearing, and then when you thought he wasn't there, there he was again, saying "I say, come on," and before you could say anything, there he wasn't.

Rabbit turned round and nudged Piglet.

"The next time," he said. "Tell Pooh."

"The next time," said Piglet to Pooh.

"The next what?" said Pooh to Piglet.

Tigger appeared suddenly, bounced into Rabbit, and disappeared again. "Now!" said Rabbit. He jumped into a hollow by the side of the path, and Pooh and Piglet jumped after him. They crouched in the bracken, listening. The Forest was very silent when you stopped and listened to it. They could see nothing and hear nothing. . . .

There was a moment's silence, and then they heard him pattering off again. For a little longer they waited, until the Forest had become so still that it almost frightened them, and then Rabbit got up and stretched himself.

"Well?" he whispered proudly. "There we are! Just as I said."

"So you got Tigger lost," said The Stranger.

"Not exactly," said Pooh. "What we didn't know was that it's a funny thing about Tiggers, they never get lost.

"Nobody knows why. They just don't. So when he couldn't find us, Tigger went right back to Kanga's and started playing with Roo. They were playing the game of throwing fir cones at each other." Pooh paused. "In case you wanted to know what they were doing."

"So you found him there, when you and Piglet and Rabbit got back," said Owl.

"Not really," said Pooh. "It went more like this."

"The fact is," said Rabbit, "we've missed our way somehow."

They were having a rest in a small sand-pit on the top of the Forest. Pooh was getting rather tired of that sand-pit, and suspected it of following them about, because whichever direction they started in, they always ended up at it, and each time, as it came through the mist at them, Rabbit said triumphantly, "Now I know where we are!" and Pooh said sadly, "So do I," and Piglet said nothing. He had tried to think of something to say, but the only thing he could think of was, "Help, help!"

and it seemed silly to say that, when he had Pooh and Rabbit with him.

"Well," said Rabbit, after a long silence in which nobody thanked him for the nice walk they were having, "we'd better get on, I suppose. Which way shall we try?"

"How would it be," said Pooh slowly, "if, as soon as we're out of sight of this Pit, we try to find it again?"

"What's the good of that?" said Rabbit.

"Well," said Pooh, "we keep looking for Home and not finding it, so I thought that if we looked for this Pit, we'd be sure not to find it, which would be a Good Thing, because then we might find something that we *weren't* looking for, which might be just what we *were* looking for, really."

"So you were lost," said The Stranger.

"Well," said Pooh. "We knew where we were, and I suppose if you know where you are, you can't very well be lost. What we didn't know was where home was."

"I assume," said Owl, "that since you are here, you eventually found where home was."

"Sort of," said Pooh. "Christopher Robin came looking and found Piglet and me and took us home and we all had a little something."

"What happened to Rabbit?" asked The Stranger.

"He had gotten separated from us and was lost, but we didn't worry because Christopher Robin said he expected that Tigger would find him since he was sort of looking for us all."

Tigger was tearing round the Forest making loud yapping noises for Rabbit. And at last a very Small and Sorry Rabbit heard him. And the Small and Sorry Rabbit rushed through the mist at the noise, and it suddenly turned into Tigger; a Friendly Tigger, a Grand Tigger, a Large and Helpful Tigger, a Tigger who bounced, if he bounced at all, in just the beautiful way a Tigger ought to bounce.

"Oh, Tigger, I *am* glad to see you," cried Rabbit.

"So the adventure ended happily," said The Stranger, "but Tigger wasn't changed. He was still Bouncy."

"Yes," said Pooh. "After that, though, nobody much minded. Especially Rabbit."

"It is very, very difficult to change someone," said The Stranger, "as we said earlier. In addition, even if we could, we would probably prefer the person the way he was, as your story shows."

"But if you can't change people," asked Owl, "how does the manager carry out her responsibility of developing people?"

"That's the funny thing about this function of a manager. You see, the manager really can't develop people. It just can't be done. All she can do is to provide an environment that encourages them to develop themselves."

" 'Hows' are difficult," said Pooh, slowly shaking his head from side to side. "This seems the most difficult 'How' of all. The manager has to develop her people, but you can't develop people."

"She can't do it directly, but there is a great deal she can do indirectly. First she must know her people. She should talk to them, observe them, and, above all, listen to them. By doing that, she will begin to learn their strengths and weaknesses.

"Once she knows those, she can start to work with the individuals. She can give assignments to them, delegate some of her own work, for instance, where their strengths will help them to perform well.

"In the process, their weaknesses will show up. They will make mistakes. However, and this is extremely important, the manager should emphasize their strengths and view their mistakes in a positive way, pointing out that mistakes are a natural part of the learning experience.

"Working under these conditions, most people will want to correct their weaknesses and will work hard to do so. The important thing is that it is done on their own, not imposed from outside. No one likes to have someone continually pointing out their weaknesses."

"What else can the manager do?" asked Pooh.

"She should select her people carefully and give them work to do that will meet their needs and that is compatible with their talents, experience, and ability. She also can provide them with appropriate training if they want to take it to upgrade their skills.

"Above all, she should leave them alone. Get out of the way and let them get on with the job. Guide them, help them, but don't sit on them or smother them."

"I sat on Piglet once," said Pooh. "By accident. He didn't much care for it."

"Few do," said Owl.

"That's exactly right," said The Stranger. "Few of us like to be hovered over. By letting her people alone, unless they need help, the manager is showing that she trusts them and considers them to be competent, mature individuals. Not everyone will respond to that, but enough of any manager's people will react favorably so that a very effective operation will be possible.

"Remember that the manager's objective is for each individual to achieve excellence within the limits of his or her talents and abilities. Once the manager makes it plain that excellence is the objective, her people will strive for it themselves. Everyone likes to be a winner, and most people like to be challenged—as long as the challenge is seen to be achievable."

"Is there any more?" asked Pooh. "Or is it lunchtime?"

"There is one other thing that we should stress. The key word in our definition of the function of developing people is 'systematically.' Since the manager is attempting to reach her objective by establishing an environment or a climate that encourages growth and improvement of the individual, she must make certain that her efforts are consistent and continuous."

"I can see that," said Owl. "If the manager's efforts

are sporadic, the ambiance will be one of change and uncertainty, obviating the idea of a consistent condition surrounding and effecting the development of an organism, namely, the individual."

"What?" said Pooh, and even The Stranger had to think about what Owl had said for a few moments.

"That's exactly right, Owl," The Stranger said finally. "Growing and improving is a process that takes place over a long period of time. The individuals must know that their efforts will be rewarded at the end of that time. The environment that will do that must be a stable one that they can count on.

"And speaking of rewards, the manager should compliment individuals, preferably in public, when they do a good job in terms of their talents and abilities. Raises and promotions come along relatively infrequently, but the opportunity to congratulate someone on doing something well occurs almost daily. The manager should seize every opportunity. The compliments will reinforce her commitment to growth and encourage the individual."

"What about the manager?" asked Pooh. "She was supposed to grow and improve her performance also."

"That's a little easier," said The Stranger. "She has control over that herself. Ideally, her superior will be doing the same thing the manager is doing with her people, but even if he does not, the manager can take on the job herself. In fact, it is vital that she do so. Do you know why?"

Pooh thought for a moment. "Because," he said slowly, "when . . . we . . . were . . . talking . . . about . . . communication, we agreed that actions speak louder than words," he finished in a rush.

"Precisely. By making efforts to grow and improve her own performance, she shows her people that she considers it to be important, which also helps to create a consistent environment. Very good, Pooh."

"I try," said Pooh modestly. "But how does the manager do it for herself?"

"First, she monitors her own performance so that she can see where she needs improvement. I think one of the best ways I've found is that used by Benjamin Franklin. In his autobiography, he tells about how he decided what qualities and skills he needed in order to become successful. He made up a checklist showing each one. Then, at the end of each day, he would review the list and give himself a mark on how well he had done that day on each item. By doing this, he not only kept reminding himself what was important, he also had a running record of his progress. I've found it very helpful, and it only takes about five minutes at the end of the day."

"Is that what you meant by 'systematically'?" asked Pooh.

"Yes. In addition, the manager should decide what skills and characteristics she might need in the future and begin to learn and practice those. Often she can get an idea as to what these should be by observing and talking to her superior. She can take extension courses, and she also can volunteer for duties that her superior does and ask that they be delegated to her."

"So the manager improves her performance on the job she is doing at the present time," said Owl, "and at the same time prepares herself for her future responsibilities."

"Exactly," said The Stranger. He looked up at the sun. "Do you know, I think we've almost gone through lunchtime."

"I know," said Pooh. "My stomach told me."

VIII

IN WHICH Pooh and The Stranger Talk About the Horrible Heffalump Trap for Managers and What They Can Do to Avoid Falling into It

While Pooh, Owl, and The Stranger were eating lunch, the weather had changed. The sun was covered by clouds, and it grew quite dark outside Pooh's house. The wind blew harder and whistled in through the crack in the door, bringing with it the scent of rain.

"I think," said Owl, licking off the last bits of bread and honey that The Stranger had thoughtfully brought, "that it might well be an auspicious time for me to return to my abode before atmospheric conditions deteriorate still further."

Pooh suggested to Owl that he had better think about going home, because it looked as if it might rain.

The Stranger looked out the door and said that it looked as if it were raining already in the direction he needed to go, so if Pooh didn't mind, he'd stay around for a little while to see if the rain would pass by.

Pooh said he didn't mind at all, as he had some questions he wanted to ask.

While Pooh cleaned up after lunch, carefully leaving out the remaining little snacks from the picnic basket, he thought about the questions he wanted to ask The Stranger, who was taking a few winks in Pooh's most comfortable chair in front of the toasty fire.

The Stranger woke up just as Pooh was finishing.

"It seems to me," Pooh said, "that a manager has ever so much to do, what with Establishing Objectives and Organizing and all the rest, that I don't see how it all gets done."

The Stranger chuckled. "I'm sure most managers would agree with you. It is a big job, and the only way that someone can do it well is to be as effective as possible."

"What's 'defective'? Is that someone who works for the police? Christopher Robin once read a book about a—a—a one of those."

"You're thinking about 'detective'—someone who investigates crime. The word I used was 'effective.' It simply means that the manager must get the right things done."

Pooh thought for a minute. Finally he said, "I see. If the manager isn't getting the right things done, then he must be getting the wrong things done, and if he gets the wrong things done, then the manager won't be making progress toward achieving his objectives. That seems simple, I think."

"That's exactly right, Pooh, but you would be surprised how often managers concentrate on the wrong things simply because they haven't thought about being effective. Many managers let themselves get distracted by tasks that will not make a major contribution toward achieving their objectives and then complain because they do not have enough time to do the important things.

"A manager should always remember what he is trying to achieve and what tasks are really important in reaching his goals. Then he should concentrate on those tasks."

"It's not always easy not to be distracted," said Pooh. "Sometimes things happen. Like the time that Piglet and I were searching for Small, one of Rabbit's friends-and-relations who was lost."

"What happened to distract you?" asked The Stranger.

"Well, it all started when Rabbit told me that Small had disappeared and that everyone had been Organized into a Search. I was to search by the Six Pine Trees first and then work my way back to Owl's House where Rabbit would meet me."

As soon as Rabbit was out of sight, Pooh remembered that he had forgotten to ask who Small was, and whether he was the sort of friend-and-relation who settled on one's nose, or the sort who got trodden on by mistake, and as it was Too Late Now, he thought he

would begin the Hunt by looking for Piglet, and asking
him what they were looking for before he looked for it.

"That seems wise," commented The Stranger.

"I thought so. It's ever so helpful to know what you
are looking for if you are looking for something. It helps
you to recognize it when you find it. I even made up a
list of How I should go about it."

ORDER OF LOOKING FOR THINGS

1. **Special Place.** (*To find Piglet.*)
2. **Piglet.** (*To find who Small is.*)
3. **Small.** (*To find Small.*)
4. **Rabbit.** (*To tell him I've found Small.*)
5. **Small Again.** (*To tell him I've found Rabbit.*)

"That's a good habit for a manager to acquire," said
The Stranger.

"Yes," said Pooh, "probably most V.I.B.s keep lists. I
was so busy writing this down in my head and not looking where I was going that I got distracted."

"Did someone interrupt you?" asked The Stranger.

"No," said Pooh. "It happened like this."

The next moment the day became very bothering
indeed, because Pooh was so busy not looking where he

was going that he stepped on a piece of the Forest which had been left out by mistake; and he only just had time to think to himself: "I'm flying. What Owl does. I wonder how you stop—" when he stopped.

Bump!

"Ow!" squeaked something.

"That's funny," thought Pooh. "I said 'Ow!' without really oo'ing."

"Help!" said a small, high voice.

"That's me again," thought Pooh. "I've had an Accident, and fallen down a well, and my voice has gone all squeaky and works before I'm ready for it, because I've done something to myself inside. Bother!"

"Help—help!"

"There you are! I say things when I'm not trying. So it must be a very bad Accident." And then he thought that perhaps when he did try to say things he wouldn't be able to; so, to make sure, he said loudly: "A Very Bad Accident to Pooh Bear."

"Pooh!" squeaked the voice.

"It's Piglet!" cried Pooh eagerly. "Where are you?"

"Underneath," said Piglet in an underneath sort of way.

"Underneath what?"

"You," squeaked Piglet. "Get up! . . ."

"What's happened?" said Pooh. "Where are we?"

"I think we're in a sort of Pit. I was walking along, looking for somebody, and then suddenly I wasn't any more, and just when I got up to see where I was, something fell on me. And it was you."

"So it was," said Pooh.

"Yes," said Piglet. "Pooh," he went on nervously, and came a little closer, "do you think we're in a trap?"

Pooh hadn't thought about it at all, but now he nodded. For suddenly he remembered how he and Piglet had once made a Pooh Trap for Heffalumps, and he guessed what had happened. He and Piglet had fallen into a Heffalump Trap for Poohs! That was what it was.

"I can see where that would be distracting," said The Stranger.

"It was," said Pooh. "Very. We spent a great deal of time Not Searching for Small because we were trying to decide what to do when the Horrible Heffalump came by to inspect his Trap for Poohs and found us in it."

"What happened when the Heffalump did find you in its Trap?"

"It didn't."

Christopher Robin, who was thinking of something else, said: "Where's Pooh?"—but Rabbit had gone. So he went into his house and drew a picture of Pooh going a long walk at about seven o'clock in the morning, and then he climbed to the top of his tree and climbed down again, and then he wondered what Pooh was doing, and went across the Forest to see.

It was not long before he came to the Gravel Pit, and he looked down, and there were Pooh and Piglet, with their backs to him, dreaming happily. . . .

"Hallo, Pooh."

Piglet looked up, and looked away again. And he felt so Foolish and Uncomfortable that he had almost decided to run away to Sea and be a Sailor . . .

"So all the time you and Piglet spent deciding what to do when the Heffalump came could have been spent on getting out of the Gravel Pit and then carrying out your Search for Small."

"Yes," said Pooh. "But we were distracted. I'm afraid I was not a Very Effective Bear."

"Still," said The Stranger, "it's a good lesson for managers. If they are to be effective, they must force themselves to set priorities and not allow themselves to be distracted. They must stay with their priority decisions. They must do first things first and second things not at all. They must be alert not to fall into the Horrible Heffalump Trap of being distracted from accomplishing their priority tasks."

"I understand that," said Pooh. "Is there anything else that a manager must do in order to be effective other than setting priorities and then sticking to them?"

"There are several. But probably the most important

thing that a manager must do in order to be effective is to manage time properly."

"How is that done?" asked Pooh, in a puzzled tone of voice. "Time just goes by. It doesn't seem to me that you can change it."

"That's very true. Everyone has the same amount of time, twenty-four hours in a day. However, some people manage to accomplish a great deal in those twenty-four hours and others very little. The reason for the difference is that those who accomplish a lot devote their time to tasks that will help them to meet their objectives—to productive tasks. They do this by eliminating or reducing as much as possible unproductive demands on their time."

"How do they do that?"

"The starting point should be for the manager to find out how he spends his time. What he is actually doing—what tasks he is performing at the present and how much time is devoted to them. He does this by keeping a record of how he spends his time each day for about a month. He records what he does as he does it and how much time it took to do it. This is called a 'Time Log,' and it is a good idea for a manager to keep one about every six months, simply because the work a manager does will change.

"The manager then can analyze his Time Log and eliminate or reduce the time spent on work that does not contribute to his priority tasks and objectives."

"How does he do that?" asked Pooh.

"Many techniques can be used. Two good books on the subject are *The Effective Executive* by Peter F. Drucker and *How to Get Control of Your Time and Your Life* by Alan Lakein.

"Finally, the manager should schedule the time available to him. A good way to do this is to sit down at a time when he will be undisturbed, say on a Sunday evening, or the first thing Monday morning, with an appointment book and think about what needs to be accomplished in the coming week.

"He should first consider his priority items and schedule blocks of time to work on them. Care must be taken not to schedule too much of the time available. If someone overschedules, he will get discouraged because he can't accomplish what was scheduled. Every manager knows that there are always interruptions and unscheduled events, so count on it in advance. Schedule only about 60 percent of the time. Leave the rest open. If nothing occurs, the manager can always rejuggle or expand the time scheduled on priority items.

"Then each day, either at the end of the day or first thing in the morning, he should review and adjust the schedule for the upcoming day and the rest of the week."

"It seems to me," said Pooh, "that the scheduling would take a lot of time, all by itself."

"Not really. After you are used to doing it, you would find that only about a half an hour is required for the weekly scheduling and about five minutes for the daily review and adjustment."

"That doesn't seem like a lot of time," said Pooh. "That's only about the amount of time in a week that I spend each day for a little afternoon snack, which normally would be scheduled right about now."

"Well," said The Stranger, walking over to the window and looking out, "a good manager doesn't deviate from the schedule unless it is absolutely necessary. The rain has passed over, and it's about time for me to be leaving. Let's have the scheduled snack and then I must be on my way."

"There are a few things left over from the picnic basket you brought. If we had them for a Little Something, then the basket would be lighter for you to carry," suggested Pooh most helpfully.

The Stranger agreed and they sat down to have a Little Something, which turned out to be a Large Something.

As they were eating The Stranger asked Pooh: "When you told me your story about the Search for Small, you never said if Small was found."

"Oh yes, I forgot. Just when Christopher Robin came along, I was trying to soothe myself in that awkward place in the middle of the back where something was tickling me when suddenly Piglet gave a shout."

"Pooh!" he cried. "There's something climbing up your back."

"I thought there was," said Pooh.

"It's Small!" cried Piglet.

"Oh, *that's* who it is, is it?" said Pooh.

"Christopher Robin, I've found Small!" cried Piglet.

"Well done, Piglet," said Christopher Robin.

IX

IN WHICH The Stranger Comes to the
Forest for the Last Time, a Party Is Held,
Pooh Becomes a Very Important Bear,
and an Enchanted Place Is Visited

Everyone knew that The Stranger would be visiting the
Forest for the last time and that there would be a party.
No one was quite sure how they knew this.

Piglet was absolutely and positively certain that he
had heard it from Rabbit, and Rabbit was equally sure that
Piglet had told him. Owl claimed to have picked up the
news from the wind that sighed softly through the trees.

Kanga was told by Roo, who was so excited at the idea
of a party that he completely forgot who had told him.

Tigger said that he just knew. "Tiggers always know
about things like that," he said. "Tiggers are very good
at knowing."

Pooh knew. He thought that The Stranger had told
him just before he left on the day it had rained, but then
again, he wasn't sure, since they had talked so much
that day that his brain had gotten tired and refused to

remember exactly what The Stranger had said. When he woke up the morning of the party, he lay in bed and tried to remember how he knew.

Knowing made Pooh feel sad. He liked having The Stranger visit the Forest because The Stranger treated him like a Bear of Some Brain instead of a Bear of Little Brain. He also liked the picnic baskets that The Stranger brought, or rather, what was inside the baskets.

Thinking about the picnic baskets reminded him about the party, which made him feel glad. Since The Stranger had brought such good food in the picnic baskets, the food for the party should be even better, since parties are supposed to be Special.

"Let's see now," he said to himself, since no one else was around, "there will probably be a pot, no, two pots of honey. Or will there be three?"

That was a difficult question and Pooh finally decided that the correct number was probably three.

"Then there are sure to be some of those little cake things with Pink Sugar icing. Maybe even enough so that one can have More if one is so inclined. Then for dessert there will be honeycombs that are nice and chewy and lots and lots of orange marmalade to spread on them to make them go down even easier—" and Pooh happily dreamed on.

Even Eeyore knew. "Someone must have made a mistake," he said gloomily. "Mostly no one tells me what is happening until it's Too Late. That's sad, but it's just the way things are. Probably there isn't going to be a party. I'll go and when I get there everyone will jump out and say 'Surprise!' and the surprise will be that there isn't a party after all. How like them.

"On the other hoof, if I don't go and there really is a party, I shall miss it. Still, I suppose they would be sending me down the odd bits that got trodden on. Kind and Thoughtful."

In the end, Eeyore decided to attend. He and the others got ready. Eeyore had considerable difficulty getting the bow on his tail tied exactly right since his tail kept acting like it was once again thinking about becoming a bell-pull, but in the end, he managed it.

Owl took particular care and made certain that his claws were spotless and well polished. After all, his contribution to the book The Stranger was writing was indubitably of inestimable value, and it was not inconceivable that the festivities were conceived to give recognition to his preoption to inscribe the dedication of the tome.

Piglet actually considered washing before he went to the party. He thought about it for a long time and then decided that if he did so, it was quite likely that no one would recognize him, and he would not be allowed to attend. So he didn't. Wash, that is.

Kanga gave Roo a thorough bath, even including washing inside his ears. For once, Roo didn't splash, but sat quietly thinking about the party. When Kanga finished, there weren't even any puddles on the  floor except for one very small one that hardly counted.

Rabbit was wondering if he should invite all his friends-and-relations. The Stranger might not be expecting that many and might not have brought enough chairs.

Finally he decided that if he didn't invite them, they would probably all come anyway. They could spread themselves on the grass and wait hopefully in case anybody spoke to them, or dropped anything, or asked them the time.

While Roo was being dried off, Tigger carefully groomed himself, licking his fur until it all lay down in exactly the right place and shone silkily in the sunlight. Tigger admired himself in the mirror after he had finished, commenting "Tiggers are very good at looking well groomed."

Pooh, deciding he had dreamed about the food that would be at the party long enough and that he had better get ready for the real thing just to see if he had dreamed it correctly, got up and carefully brushed his fur into place. It had gotten all

scrambled while he slept and didn't look at all like the Fur of a Bear Who Is Going to a Party.

Finally everyone was ready and found their way to where a long table and chairs had been set up at the base of one of the largest trees in the Forest. Even Eeyore arrived on time, saying "Don't blame me if it rains."

It didn't rain. It was, in fact, a beautiful, warm, sunny day. The earlier rains had washed everything clean, and the leaves shone as they nodded and fluttered in the soft, gentle breezes that whispered through the Forest. Little spots of sunlight danced across the food, which covered every inch of the table.

There was everything that Pooh had dreamed about and more. There was even enough so that all of Rabbit's friends-and-relations did not have to depend on What Someone Might Carelessly Drop. There were specially succulent thistles fresh cut for Eeyore, haycorns for Piglet, Extract of Malt for Tigger, and plenty of honey, bread, and condensed milk for everyone. And little cake things with Pink Sugar icing, of course.

When they all had eaten nearly enough, and then some more, The Stranger stood up and made a speech. He told them nicely how much he appreciated their contribution to his book.

"Contri—what?" asked Pooh.

"Hush," said Owl. "What you told him."

"Oh," said Pooh.

He said he was sorry to be leaving, but that he

would come back to the Forest someday. Then The Stranger thanked everyone by name, even Small, and told them He Could Not Have Done It Without Them.

Everyone clapped and then Eeyore and Owl both began to make a speech at the same time; Owl starting "Unaccustomed as I am—" and Eeyore beginning "At least it didn't rain—yet." Since each was listening only to his own speech, they both continued, which made it very difficult for those around the table to understand what either one was saying.

It didn't really matter, however, because it was a good time to have just a little smidgen more of your favorite Whatever. Pooh had two Mores of the little cake things with Pink Sugar icing.

When the Owl/Eeyore speech was over and everyone had clapped enough, Pooh stood up.

"When you first came to the Forest," he said, looking at The Stranger, "I fear I was a Bear of Very Little Brain, particularly about Management. Now I know a little about it and about what a manager should do in order to be a Good Manager. You even very carefully explained the 'Hows' so that I could understand them." Pooh shook his head. "I have always had difficulty with 'Hows.' 'Whats' are not nearly as hard."

"Tiggers are Very Good at 'Hows,'" said Tigger in a muffled, faraway-under-the-table kind of voice.

"Yes," said Pooh, wondering where Tigger had gotten to. "But I also think I understand a 'Why.' I think I understand why a manager is."

"Why is a manager?" asked The Stranger.

"It's like when I went visiting Rabbit one day after I had finished doing my Stoutness Exercises in front of the mirror. Because of Rabbit's hospitality, I ate too much." Pooh patted his stomach. "Almost as much as today, and when I tried to go home, I got stuck in Rabbit's front door, which was wide enough going in but too narrow when one wanted to come out."

"So what happened then?" asked The Stranger.

"Rabbit told me what the Trouble was."

"The fact is," said Rabbit, "you're stuck."

"It all comes," said Pooh crossly, "of not having front doors big enough."

"It all comes," said Rabbit sternly, "of eating too much. I thought at the time," said Rabbit, "only I didn't like to say anything," said Rabbit, "that one of us was eating too much," said Rabbit, "and I knew it wasn't *me*," he said. "Well, well, I shall go and fetch Christopher Robin. . . ."

Christopher Robin nodded.

"Then there's only one thing to be done," he said. "We shall have to wait for you to get thin again."

"How long does getting thin take?" asked Pooh anxiously.

"About a week, I should think."

"But I can't stay here for a *week*!"

"You can *stay* here all right, silly old Bear. It's getting you out which is so difficult."

"We'll read to you," said Rabbit cheerfully. "And I hope it won't snow," he added. "And I say, old fellow, you're taking up a good deal of room in my house—*do* you mind if I use your back legs as a towel-horse? Because, I mean, there they are—doing nothing—and it would be very convenient just to hang the towels on them."

"A week!" said Pooh gloomily. "*What about meals?*"

"I'm afraid no meals," said Christopher Robin, "because of getting thin quicker. But we *will* read to you."

Bear began to sigh, and then found he couldn't because he was so tightly stuck; and a tear rolled down his eye, as he said:

"Then would you read a Sustaining Book, such as would help and comfort a Wedged Bear in Great Tightness?"

So for a week Christopher Robin read that sort of book at the North end of Pooh, and Rabbit hung his washing on the South end . . . and in between Bear felt himself getting slenderer and slenderer. And at the end of the week Christopher Robin said, *"Now!"*

So he took hold of Pooh's front paws and Rabbit took hold of Christopher Robin, and all Rabbit's friends and relations took hold of Rabbit, and they all pulled together. . . .

And for a long time Pooh only said *"Ow!"* . . .

And *"Oh!"* . . .

And then, all of a sudden, he said *"Pop!"* just as if a cork were coming out of a bottle.

And Christopher Robin and Rabbit and all Rabbit's friends and relations went head-over-heels backwards . . . and on the top of them came Winnie-the-Pooh—free!

"And that's why a manager is," said Pooh.

"To get you out of tight places when you eat too much?" asked Eeyore.

"No," said Pooh. "To get everyone to pull together in order to accomplish an objective."

Afterward, when everyone except Pooh and The Stranger had gone home and all the cleaning up had been done, The Stranger suggested that they take a little walk to work off some of the Fullness.

They walked along, not talking very much, except things like "The pink icing was unusually good, wasn't it?" and "Everyone made good speeches, didn't they?" until at last they came to an enchanted place on the very top of the Forest called Galleons Lap where Pooh had gone once before, a long time ago, with Christopher Robin before he went away.

The place was indeed enchanted. Its floor was close-set grass, quiet and smooth and green. It was still the only place in the Forest where you could sit down care-

lessly, without getting up again almost at once and looking for someplace else.

No one could count the sixty-odd trees that surrounded the glade in a circle. Sitting there, Pooh and The Stranger could see the whole world spread out until it reached the sky.

In the enchanted place, everything seemed to be very simple and easy to understand, even management, and somehow, accomplishing anything that

one wanted to accomplish did not appear to be at all difficult.

Pooh sat quietly, his back against one of the trees, and thought about all that The Stranger and he had talked about.

"Do you think I might?" he finally asked.

"Might what, Pooh?"

"Do you think I might really become a Very Important Bear since I helped you with a Very Important Subject like Management? If your book gets published, that is."

"Pooh, in my opinion, it doesn't matter if my book gets published or not, you always have been, are, and always will be a Very, Very Important Bear."

"Oh," thought Pooh. "That sort of Bear!"

X

IN WHICH The Stranger Thinks About Visiting the Forest, What Was Found There, and What Was Brought Back

The Stranger leaned back in his comfortable armchair, which was placed at exactly the right distance from the Very Nice Fire burning on the hearth. Outside it was a rainy, blusterous sort of day that made the fire seem even cozier and caused the flames to flare up from time to time and then settle back and crackle quietly to itself.

One might, if one had to be outdoors and struggle with a turned-inside-out umbrella and cold rain trickling down the back of a neck, be inclined to say that this was not a Friendly Day. But indoors, with all your work done, a comforting fire, an easy chair, a little something from the kitchen on the table beside you, and a Very Good Book, it was a Perfect Day. A day just made to think and dream and maybe even nap a little.

The Stranger was thinking about the Forest where

Winnie-the-Pooh and his friends lived. At first glance, it seemed a far different world from our everyday one of mind-boggling change, constant crises, confrontations, insecurity, stress, and ephemeral morality.

However, that is only the way it seemed. "Pooh's world is actually much like ours," The Stranger thought. What could be more stressful than to be caught in a Horrible Heffalump Trap? Imagine the insecurity of being down to your last pot of honey with no bee-tree in sight or the unsettling change of having Strange Animals, who are generally regarded as one of the Fiercer Animals, move into your neighborhood.

Visiting the Forest, The Stranger found that their adventures could be used to illustrate and emphasize managerial skills that could be applied equally well to their problems and ours. The "Hows" of the six functions a manager needs to perform are universal: Establishing objectives; organizing; communicating; developing people; motivating; and measurement and analysis are applicable to any field of endeavor—an Expotition to the North Pole, business, the public sector, volunteer work, professions, or one's private life.

In the Forest, however, problems somehow do not seem as complex or the consequences as serious as those we face. Besides, in the Hundred Acre Wood, there is always the comforting thought that Christopher Robin will come along to set things straight if All Else Fails.

In our society, we can't always count on a Christopher Robin standing in the wings waiting to help. We need to rely on our own and our collective talents, abilities, and resources. Excellent managers are needed, and the need will be even greater in the future.

Having problems and difficulties is the nature of life and the reason we need excellent managers. Mastery of the six functions of the manager's job will not eliminate the problems, but it will ensure that on the journey through the Forest, there will be fewer gorse-bushes and thistles along the way and ambushes will be encountered less frequently.

Those who strive for excellence will help us all to meet the challenges the future will bring.

"So," The Stranger thought, "we should begin now. It is never too early to start, and every single one of us can improve our performance if we really want to. There is an old Chinese saying that 'Not to advance is to fall behind.'

"Start now with Benjamin Franklin's checklist and begin to move toward excellence as a manager."

The Stranger relaxed. He was comfortable with what he had brought back from his visit to the Forest. He knew that Pooh would wish everyone well in their efforts to improve.

And, after all, what could be more conducive to success than to have on your side as guide and inspiration a V.I.B. like Winnie-the-Pooh?